TEXTUAL CRITICISM

WORKBOOK

The Credo Courses

ISBN: 0615927122
ISBN-13: 978-0615927121

Printed in the United States of America.

TABLE OF CONTENTS

TABLE OF CONTENTS

SESSION #1

INTRODUCTION TO NEW TESTAMENT TEXTUAL CRITICISM

TEXTUAL CRITICISM

Overview

- Materials and Methods
- Definition and Goal
- How to count textual variants
- The Number of Variants
- The Nature of Variants
- Recent attempts to change the goal

Materials and Methods in Making Ancient Books

- History of the Transmission of the Text

- Illustrations of Scribal Corruptions: Unintentional Changes

- Illustrations of Scribal Corruptions: Intentional Changes

- Some Famous Manuscripts

    P52

    Chester Beatty Papyri

    Bodmer Papyri

    Codex Vaticanus & Codex Sinaiticus

    Codex Alexandrinus & Codex Ephraemi Rescriptus

    Codex Bezae

    Codex Washingtonianus

- Resources for NT Manuscripts

- Institute for New Testament Textual Criticism

- British Library: Sinaiticus and Alexandrinus

- Evangelical Textual Criticism

- Center for the Study of New Testament Manuscripts

Methods for Doing New Testament Textual Criticism

- The Greek Text Behind the KJV: Part 1

- The Greek Text Behind the KJV: Part 2

- The Textus Receptus and the Doctrine of Preservation

- History of the Discipline Since the TR

- Tischendorf and the Discovery of Sinaiticus

- Westcott-Hort and the Dethroning of the TR

- Methods for Doing NTTC (continued)

- Principles of Reasoned Eclecticism: Part 1

- Principles of Reasoned Eclecticism: Part 2

- Principles of Reasoned Eclecticism: Part 3

Some Famous Textual Problems

1 Timothy 3.16 & John 1.18

Matthew 24.36

Mark 1.41

Matthew 27.16–17

Romans 5.1 and 8.1

Luke 22.43–44

Luke 23.34a

John 5.3b–4

1 Thessalonians 2.7

Jude 5

Revelation 13.18

Mark 16.9–20

John 7.53–8.11

Results of doing New Testament Textual Criticism: Is what we have now what they wrote then?

Definition and Goal of NT Textual Criticism

In general: The study of the copies of any written document whose original (=the autograph) is unknown or non-existent, for the primary purpose of determining the exact wording of the original.

For the New Testament: The study of the handwritten copies of the New Testament whose original (=the autograph) is unknown or non-existent, for the primary purpose of determining the exact wording of the original.

- The autographs no longer exist.

- There are differences among the copies.

- If we still had the autographs, TC would not be necessary.

- If the copies were exactly alike, TC would not be possible.

Why New Testament Textual Criticism is Necessary?

- In this respect, NTTC is no different from the textual criticism for any other major religion.

Even the Qur'an manuscripts have errors in them (thought not admitted by Muslims).

Secondary Objective

- To trace the changes to the text in various places and times to gain a window on the shape of ancient Christianity.

- We need to distinguish between MSS of the NT and MSS of other early 'Christian' writings.

- For the most part, other early Christian writings are far more corrupt than NT MSS.

For example: The *Gospel of Thomas* had major textual upheavals, as seen by the four MSS of Thomas we have today.

- For more information, see Timothy Ricchuiti, *"Tracking Thomas: A Text-Critical Look at the Transmission of the Gospel of Thomas,"* chapter 5 in *Revisiting the Corruption of the New Testament: Manuscript, Patristic, and Apocryphal Evidence*, ed. D. B. Wallace (Grand Rapids: Kregel, 2011)

- Until a few years ago, everyone thought they knew what 'original text' meant.

1999: Eldon Epp, "The Multivalence of the Term "Original Text" in New Testament Textual Criticism," *Harvard Theological Review* 92 (1999) 245–81.

Epp gives several different definitions:

- Predecessor text-form: one form of the text before it was published

- Autographic text-form: the form of the text when dispatched from the author

• Canonical text-form: the form of the text when NT books became 'canonical'

• Interpretive text-form: the form of the text in a given locale with interpretive alterations to the text

• The common-sense approach is to embrace definition #2:

• The document that left the author's hands as it was dispatched to the primary readers

• The last stage of the text while under the author's control

• Also known as the 'autographic text,' the 'autograph(s),' or the Ausgangstext. This is what we mean when speaking of the 'original text.'

SESSION #2

HOW TO COUNT TEXTUAL VARIANTS

TEXTUAL CRITICISM

How not to count variants:

"Some have estimated there are about 200,000 [textual variants]. First of all, these are not 'errors' but variant readings, the vast majority of which are strictly grammatical. Second, these readings are spread throughout more than 5300 manuscripts, so that a variant spelling of one letter of one word in one verse in 2000 manuscripts is counted as 2000 'errors.'"

- (Norman Geisler, Baker Encyclopedia of Christian Apologetics Grand Rapids: Baker, 1998 532.)

Several errors in this statement:

• If the primary goal of NT textual criticism is to recover the wording of the autographs (i.e., the texts as they left the apostles' hands), then any deviation from that wording is, by definition, an error...

• The number of manuscripts (5300) is way too low.

• The estimate of 200,000 textual variants is way too low.

- The author claims that textual variants are counted by the number of manuscripts that support a variant. But the number of manuscripts is almost completely irrelevant.

How to count variants:

- A textual variant is counted by the number of wording differences found in the MSS, regardless of how many MSS have that wording.

- All that is necessary is that a variant has one MS with this wording to count.

- Whether it is one MS or 2000 that all have the same variant, it still counts as only one variant.

What was the motive for the errant view?

- This method of counting reduces the actual number of differences in wording among the MSS to a few hundred.

- It gives Christians assurance about having the Word of God in their hands today.

- But if the assurance has a faulty basis, it is no assurance at all.

Source for Miscalculation

Geisler is not alone in this miscalculation. Many apologists have made, and continue to make, the same claims.

The source seems to be a book published in 1963 called *How We Got the Bible*, by Neil Lightfoot (Grand Rapids: Baker). Reprinted and edited many times, it has sold over one million copies.

What Lightfoot wrote:

> "From one point of view it may be said that there are 200,000 scribal errors in the manuscripts, but it is wholly misleading and untrue to say that there are 200,000 errors in the text of the New Testament. This large number is gained by counting all the variations in all of the manuscripts (about 4,500). This means that if, for example, one word is misspelled in 4,000 different manuscripts, it amounts to 4,000 'errors.' Actually in a case of this kind only one slight error has been made and it has been copied 4,000 times. But this is the procedure which is followed in arriving at the large number of 200,000 'errors.'
>
> *- Neil Lightfoot, How We Got the Bible, 53–54.*

Proof of the Miscalculation

•   The Majority Text disagrees with the standard critical Greek New Testament, the Nestle-Aland Novum Testamentum Graece, in more than 6500 places.

•   On average, the Majority Text has a good 500 MSS on its side for each variant it supports.

•   If Lightfoot is right, then 6500 x 500 should not equal more than 200,000. But it's actually 3,250,000!

•   And these 6500 differences are only a small fraction of all the variants there are.

•   The Nestle-Aland Novum Testamentum Graece lists approximately 30,000 textual variants.

• A textual variant is any place where at least one MS deviates from a base text.

• Nestle-Aland lists only a small fraction of all textual variants.

If Lightfoot's method of counting variants were correct, we would have at least tens of millions of variants.

Would that number actually give anyone any assurance at all?

How to Count Textual Variants

No textual critic defines a textual variant the way that Lightfoot has done. Yet, the number of textual variants comes from textual critics. Shouldn't they be the ones to define what this means since they're the ones doing the counting?

To Recap: A textual variant is NOT a difference in wording times the number of MSS supporting the difference. It is simply any place where at least one MS differs from a base text. Regardless of how many MSS share the same variant, it still only counts as one variant.

As we will see in the next lecture, there are far more than 200,000 variants, even when properly counted.

SESSION #3

THE NUMBER OF VARIANTS OR HOW MUCH DID THE SCRIBES CORRUPT THE TEXT?

TEXTUAL CRITICISM

The Quantity of Variants

Greek NT:

c. 140,000

Textual Variants:
c.400,000

The Quantity of Variants

Greek NT: c. 140,000

The reason we have a lot of textual variants is that we have a lot of manuscripts.

Richard Bentley Remarks upon a Discourse of Free Thinking (1713)

> "If there had been but one manuscript of the Greek Testament at the restoration of learning about two centuries ago, then we [would have] had no various readings at all. … And would the text be in a better condition then, than now [that] we have 30,000 [variant readings]? It is good, therefore… to have more anchors than one; and another MS. to join the first would give more authority, as well as security."

An Embarrassment of Riches

- Greek manuscripts: 5824

- Latin manuscripts: 10,000+

- Other ancient versions: 5000–10,000

- Quotations from the New Testament by church fathers: over 1 million

The NT compared to the average classical work

The average classical Greek writer has less than 20 copies of his works still in existence. Stack them up, and they're 4 feet high.

The NT compared to the average classical work

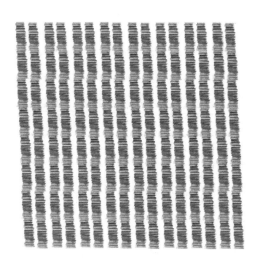

Greco-Roman Authors

- Pliny the Elder: 700 years
- Plutarch: 800 years
- Josephus: 800 years
- Polybius: 1200 years
- Pausanias: 1400 years
- Herodotus: 1500 years
- Xenophon: 1800 years

An ounce of evidence is worth a pound of presumption!

- Within 125 years of the completion of the NT, over 43% of all verses are found in the papyri.

- Within 125 years of the completion of almost all classical literature, 0% of the document is found in any manuscripts.

There are three times more NT MSS within the first 200 years than the average Greco-Roman author has in 2000 years.

Has the Bible been translated and retranslated so many times that we don't know what it originally said?

Year	Number of MSS	Earliest MSS
1611	7	11th century
2013	5800+	2nd century

The bottom line:

As time goes on, we are getting closer and closer to the original text.

.

SESSION #4

WEIGHING THE DISCREPANCIES: THE NATURE OF TEXTUAL VARIANTS

TEXTUAL CRITICISM

Four groups of textual variants

All variants can be grouped in terms of whether they are meaningful or viable.

meaningful = change the meaning of the text

viable = have a sufficient pedigree to potentially represent the wording of the original

Viable but not meaningful	Meaningful but not viable
Neither meaningful nor viable	Meaningful *and* viable

The first three groups: not meaningful, not viable, or both

Over 99% of all variants

Illustrations of viable but not meaningful variants:

Differences in spelling

the name for "John" in Greek: Ioannes or Ioanes

moveable nu...

Word order differences

How many ways are there to say:

"John loves Mary" in Greek?

1.   Ἰωάννης ἀγαπᾷ Μαρίαν
2.   Ἰωάννης ἀγαπᾷ τὴν Μαρίαν

3.   ὁ Ἰωάννης ἀγαπᾷ Μαρίαν
4.   ὁ Ἰωάννης ἀγαπᾷ τὴν Μαρίαν
5.   Μαρίαν Ἰωάννης ἀγαπᾷ
6.   τὴν Μαρίαν Ἰωάννης ἀγαπᾷ
7.   Μαρίαν ὁ Ἰωάννης ἀγαπᾷ
8.   τὴν Μαρίαν ὁ Ἰωάννης ἀγαπᾷ

These are only a few of the ways to say "John loves Mary" in Greek.

Other legitimate word orders swell the numbers to over 500

A different verb for 'loves' mushrooms the numbers to nearly 1200

"We could go on nearly forever talking about specific places in which the texts of the New Testament came to be changed, either accidentally or intentionally...the examples are not just in the hundreds but in the thousands."
                                          - Bart Ehrman, Misquoting Jesus

This is true, but irrelevant and even implicitly deceptive. The reader gets the sense that there are thousands of variants that are significant, when that is not at all the case. No one--not even the most anal textual critics--want to talk about all the variants! We'd be bored to death with the trivia.

If we can say "John loves Mary" over 1000 times in Greek without substantially changing the meaning, the number of textual variants for the NT is meaningless. What counts is the nature of the variants.

Meaningful but not viable (i.e., a poor chance of being authentic)

We the People of the United States, in Order to form a more perfect Onion...

1 Thessalonians 2.7: "although we could have imposed our weight as apostles of Christ; instead we became little children/gentle among you..."

'little children' vs. 'gentle': nepioi vs. epioi (νήπιοι vs. ἤπιοι)

one late manuscript: hippoi (ἵπποι) translated: 'horses'!

An illustration just for Greek students:

John 1.30: ὀπίσω μου ἔρχεται ἀνήρ (aner)
Codex L (8th century): ὀπίσω μου ἔρχεται ἀήρ (aer)

The smallest group of variants:

Meaningful and viable (good chance of being authentic)

Less than 1% of all textual variants

Examples of meaningful & viable variants:

Romans 8.2: "For the law of the Spirit of life in Christ Jesus has set you free from the law of sin and death."

Most MSS have me instead of you here.

Some have us instead of you.

Philippians 1.14: "and most of the brothers and sisters... now more than ever dare to speak the word fearlessly."

Several MSS add of God after the word.

Others add of the Lord after the word.

To sum up:

- Among the 400,000 textual variants in NT MSS, over 99% make virtually no difference at all.

- Less than 1% are both meaningful & viable.

- How meaningful are they? You'll have to wait for the final lecture to find out.

SESSION #5

RECENT ATTEMPTS TO CHANGE THE GOALS OF NTTC

TEXTUAL CRITICISM

Definition of goal for textual criticism of any ancient text:

> The study of the copies of any written document whose original (=the autograph) is unknown or non-existent, for the primary purpose of determining the exact wording of the original.

Until 1993, this was assumed for the NT, too.

Three major influences:

Bart Ehrman's *Orthodox Corruption of Scripture* (1993): early traditions are as important as recovering the original wording. We should not privilege the autographs.

David Parker's *Living Text of the Gospels* (1997): "Textual criticism is in essence the act of understanding what another person means by the words that are laid before me" (1).

Eldon Epp's "The Multivalence of the Term 'Original Text' in New Testament Textual Criticism," *HTR* 92 (1999) 245–81.

Two major premises:

1. At times it is impossible to recover the wording of the original text. Therefore, this should no longer be the goal.

2. The variants provide a window on church history, and this is an area that has been largely neglected by textual critics.

Eldon Epp's "The Multivalence of the Term 'Original Text' in New Testament Textual Criticism," 270:

"[R]ecognizing the multivalence of 'original text' ensures that New Testament textual criticism will certainly diminish and possibly relinquish its myopic concentration on an elusive and often illusive target of a single original text."

Parker's Living Text of the Gospels

"The book has been written with the growing conviction that, once the present approach has been adopted, much else in our understanding of the Gospels requires revision" (xi).

"Are the Gospels the kinds of texts that have originals?" (7). The rest of his book argues that they do not.

"The question is not whether we can recover [the original text], but why we want to" (209).

Arguments from Shakespeare, Mozart: "There are just different texts from different stages of production" (4). Thus, no original text.

Critique:

Authorial control vs. loss of control via dispatch

1. Copyists wanted to retain the authoritative voice of the apostles.

2. Aesthetics vs. spiritual authority

3. Parker's Living Text of the Gospels

4. Connection to divine history; thus, the autographic text should be sought

5. Artistic preferences vs. polemics

6. If the alteration of the original text takes the form of changing the meaning, then to that degree it also dilutes the authority of the original author's message.

Moisés Silva,"Response," in Rethinking New Testament Textual Criticism, ed. D. A. Black (Baker, 2002) 149. (This book included a dialogue between Eldon Epp, Michael Holmes, J. K. Elliott, Maurice Robinson, and Moisés Silva.)

Silva, "Response," 149:

> "I would like to affirm—not only with Hort, but with practically all students of ancient documents—that the recovery of the original

text... remains the primary task of textual criticism. Of course, it is not the only task. The study of early textual variation for its own sake is both a fascinating and a most profitable exercise. And it is also true that we have sometimes been sloppy in our use of the term original text. But neither of these truths nor the admittedly great difficulties involved in recovering the autographic words can be allowed to dissolve the concept of an original text. Nor do I find it helpful when David Parker for example, sanctifies his proposals by a theological appeal to a divinely inspired textual diversity—indeed, textual confusion and contradiction—that is supposed to be of greater spiritual value than apostolic authority.

But even apart from that, for us to retreat from the traditional task of textual criticism is equivalent to shooting ourselves in the foot. And my exhibit A is Bart Ehrman's brilliant monograph The Orthodox Corruption of Scripture....

Although this book is appealed to in support of blurring the notion of an original text, there is hardly a page in that book that does not in fact mention such a text or assume its accessibility.... Indeed, Ehrman's book is unimaginable unless he can identify an initial form of the text that can be differentiated from a later alteration."

General critique of the Ehrman-Parker-Epp view:

• If it's seemingly impossible to recover the exact wording of the NT in every place, not to try is a counsel of despair. Since when does the non-attainability of perfection in other endeavors mean we should throw in the towel?

• The neglect of one area in the past does not mean that we should now neglect another. Two wrongs don't make a right.

To sum up:

The primary goal of NT textual criticism, like the textual criticism of all other literature, must still be the recovery of the wording of the autographic text.

The secondary goal of gaining a window on the ancient church in various times and places must not be neglected, but it must never replace the primary objective.

SESSIONS #6 & #7

MATERIALS AND METHODS IN MAK-ING ANCIENT BOOKS

TEXTUAL CRITICISM

Two kinds of books

1. Roll (or scroll)
2. Codex

Books of the NT

All were no doubt written originally on a roll:

Hebrews

Rev 5.1: "Then I saw in the right hand of the one who was seated on the throne a scroll written on the front and back and sealed with seven seals."

Mark's Gospel

The copies of the New Testament

All but four papyri were written on codices.

Four were written on scrolls: all of them were reused scrolls, with the NT text on the verso and some other text on the recto.

No other extant NT MSS were written on scrolls.

The Making of a Codex

This involved the use of quires

A quire is one or more double leaves (bifolio), folded in the middle, and sewn into the binding.

- The earliest codices were single-quire books.

- P46 (c. 200 CE) is a single-quire codex.

- As the art of making books improved, the standard quire size became 8 leaves (4 bifolios).

- Most books from about the fourth century on used 4 bifolios per quire.

- When examining a codex, one can usually get a quick & dirty sense of how much material is still there.

Three different materials were used in making a codex:

1. papyrus
2. parchment
3. paper

Rom 5.1 in Sinaiticus:

εχωμεν in original hand

εχομεν (ο above ω) written by 'corrector'

εχωμεν: 'let us have peace'

εχομεν: 'we have peace'

Summary

• Parchment was by far the most durable material, followed by papyrus then paper.

• Knowing about the form of the book helps us to interpret the data, especially what would have been in the missing leaves.

SESSIONS #8, #9 & #10

A BRIEF HISTORY OF THE TRANSMISSION OF THE TEXT

TEXTUAL CRITICISM

Three Issues in the History of the Transmission of the Text

1. The Early Copies and the Causes of Corruption
2. The Role of the Canon in Shaping the NT Text
3. The Emergence of Local Text-forms

1. The Early Copies and the Causes of Corruption

• All manuscripts were handwritten; therefore, all scribes made mistakes

• Mistakes are of two kinds: unintentional and intentional

- The earliest scribes were not professionally trained: what kinds of mistakes did they make?

- All manuscripts were handwritten. Therefore, all scribes made mistakes.

Mistakes are of two kinds: unintentional and intentional

The earliest scribes were not professionally trained. What kinds of mistakes did they make?

Some suggest that the earliest scribes were the worst scribes because they were not professionals. And they imply that the mistakes were difficult to trace.

All three suppositions are demonstrably false:

1. Some of the earliest MSS were done very carefully, even though by unprofessional scribes.

2. Some of the earliest MSS were done by professionals, but they were not done carefully.

3. Kinds of mistakes: usually unintentional. These are easiest type to discover: "we the people of the United States..."

4. Early scribes were often bureaucrats, bean counters, CPAs. Not creative, just faithful...

But not all mistakes in the early period were unintentional.

Emerging canon consciousness in the second century: freedom

to add, subtract, change before canon settled.

NT books supplemented with personal reminiscences and hear-say: e.g., text of Acts

'Western' text-form especially was uncontrolled, missionary text

The early period shows two distinct kinds of copying: uncontrolled and controlled.

The 'Western' was largely uncontrolled, but demonstrably early.

The Alexandrian was carefully controlled, with roots deep in the second century.

This demonstrates that the age of a MS is not the only criterion of its value.

2. The Role of the Canon in Shaping the NT Text

• As canon consciousness emerged, more careful copying was done.

• Readings could sneak into the text before the text was well known in a particular form.

• However, precisely when the NT books began to be considered scripture, a certain kind of error crept in...

Errant readings borne by piety:

• harmonizations in the Gospels

• 'corrections' of supposed discrepancies

- explanatory glosses

- liturgically-motivated additions

Every Gospel MS of any substantial length has harmonizations in it.

What does this tell us about the motives of the scribes?

Illustration of scribal piety:

John 4.17: ἀπεκρίθη ἡ γυνὴ καὶ εἶπεν αὐτῷ· οὐκ ἔχω ἄνδρα. λέγει αὐτῇ ὁ Ἰησοῦς· καλῶς εἶπας ὅτι ἄνδρα οὐκ ἔχω

The woman answered and said to him, "I don't have a husband." Jesus said to her, "Correctly you have said, 'A husband I don't have.'

א C D changed the woman's words to conform to Jesus'.

3. The Emergence of Local Text-forms

Definition of 'text-type'

- Three or four text-types: Alexandrian, Western, Byzantine, Caesarean

- Nomenclature disputed today by some textual critics

- Still serviceable for understanding the transmission of the text

- Illustration: NIV, NASB, KJV sans Gutenberg

- Mixture in extant MSS means no pure MS of any text-form (except some late Byzantines)

- Illustration: Luke 24.53—"They were in the temple, {blessing/praising/blessing and praising} God"

Text-types and numerical preponderance

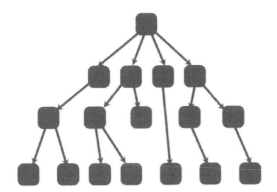
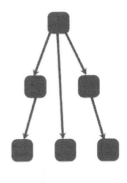

Text-types and genealogical solidarity

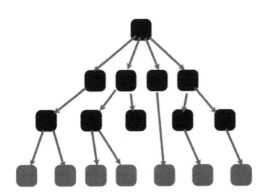
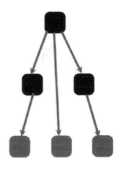

Text-types of the NT MSS

- Alexandrian
- 'Western'
- Byzantine
- Caesarean

Alexandrian: other things being equal, Alexandrian solidarity = autograph

'Western': early but erratic; strong internal evidence needed to make a claim of authenticity

Byzantine: later, secondary text, but with some authentic readings slipping through the net...

Caesarean: later, secondary text (precursor to Byzantine), but with very few authentic readings slipping through the net...

The Emerging Dominance of the Byzantine Text

- 90% of all GNT MSS are Byzantine

- How can we explain this dominance? Does majority = original?

Six Reasons for Its Dominance:

1. Diocletian persecution (303–311)

2. Constantine and Constantinople

3.   Latin as the lingua franca of the West

4.   John Chrysostom as popularizer of Byzantine Text

5.   African Christianity and the rise of Islam

6.   The Invasion of Constantinople (1453) and the Roots of the Reformation

Summary

- Only if the transmission of the text was uniform (copying frequency the same in all regions) would the majority = original.

- Six reasons why the copying frequency was not uniform

- What to count and when to count?

- Byzantine text is largely late, secondary, and inferior.

SESSION #11

ILLUSTRATIONS OF SCRIBAL CORRUPTIONS, PART 1: UNINTENTIONAL ERRORS

TEXTUAL CRITICISM

Two kinds of corruptions

1. Unintentional errors
2. Intentional changes

Importance of the classifications:

• Establishment of demonstrable scribal changes gives insight into textual problems whose solution may not be self-evident.

• Clear categories of errors become the basis for assessing possible scribal corruptions in any given instance.

- A major task in determining the wording of the autographa is to eliminate possibilities of corruption on the basis of known types and their causes.

Unintentional Errors: Six Categories

1. Sight
2. Hearing
3. Memory
4. Judgment
5. Fatigue
6. Carelessness

Errors of Sight: Three Basic Types

1. Confusion of Letters

2. Homoioteleuton (similar endings)

3. Metathesis (transposition)

Errors of Sight: Confusion of Letters

- Most discussions of letter confusion are concentrated on capital letters, since all NT MSS through the eighth century were in majuscule (or capital letter) script.

- Metzger: "It is scarcely necessary to consider similarities of letters in the subsequent minuscule script, for the overwhelming proportion of

variant readings originated prior to the period of the minuscule manuscripts."

Examples:

- Romans 6.5

- 1 Tim 3.16

Errors of Sight: Homoioteleuton

Homoioteleuton is the cause of two types of errors:

1. Haplography: writing once what should have been written twice.

2. Dittography: writing twice what should have been written once.

Most scholars regard homoioteleuton as the similar ending of lines, but
it could also be the similar ending of words on the same line.

There is also homoioarchton and homoiomeson.

Examples:

- Haplography in the Byzantine MSS of 1 John 2.23:
-"everyone who denies the Son neither has the Father; the one who
confesses the Son also has the Father"

-Byz:
"everyone who denies the Son does neither has the Father"

- Dittography in Sinaiticus in 1 Thess 2.13–14

The text should read:

> "13 And so we too constantly thank God that when you received
> God's message that you heard from us, you accepted it not as
> a human message, but as it truly is, God's message, which is at
> work among you who believe. 14 For you became imitators,
> brothers and sisters, of God's churches in Christ Jesus that are in
> Judea, because you too suffered the same things from your own
> countrymen as they in fact did from the Jews."

But the scribe's eye keyed in on the first "God's" in v. 13 (which is
eleven lines above "God's" in v. 14), and repeated the rest of that verse
before catching his mistake.

Verse 14 thus reads:

> "For you became imitators, brothers and sisters, of God's [back to
> v. 13!] message that you heard from us, you accepted it not as a hu-
> man message..."

Errors of Sight: Metathesis (Transposition)

- Switching the order of letters, words, or phrases.

- The habits of a particular MS indicate how the scribe copied. E.g.,
codex Bezae, P75.

- Incidental note on a scribe's proficiency in Greek and the quality of
his MS.

- Mark 14.65: οἱ ὑπηρέται ῥαπίσμασιν αὐτὸν ἔλαβον ("the servant
received him with many blows").

- οἱ ὑπηρέται ῥαπίσμασιν αὐτὸν ἔβαλον ("the servant struck him with many blows").

- The difference is between elabon and ebalon.

Errors of Hearing

Hearing errors have often been suggested for the MSS.

However, this presupposes that the scribes worked in a scriptorium with a reader pronouncing out the words for scribes to copy. The evidence that this happened is virtually non-existent. Nevertheless, reading in the ancient world was almost always out loud. A scribe would look at the text, read it out loud, remember it, and copy it.

If he read it or remembered it incorrectly, he would write it incorrectly.

Also, the amanuensis might incorrectly hear the author dictate it. Two passages especially seem to fit this:

1. Rom 5.1: "we have peace with God" or "let us have peace with God"

   Difference is one letter in Greek:
   εχομεν vs. εχωμεν (echomen vs. echomen)

   Rom 5.1 in Sinaiticus:
   - εχωμεν in original hand
   - εχομεν (ο above ω) written by 'corrector':

- εχωμεν: 'let us have peace'

- εχομεν: 'we have peace'

2. 1 Thessalonians 2.7: "...although we could have imposed our weight as apostles of Christ; instead we became little children/gentle among you..."

- 'little children' vs. 'gentle': nepioi vs. epioi
- νήπιοι vs. ἤπιοι
- previous word ends in a nu: egenethemen (ἐγενήθημεν)

How to solve this problem?

Errors of Memory

Errors of memory were often responsible for:

- the substitution of synonyms

- transposition of words

- transposition of letters

- assimilation of one passage to another, more familiar one (though this was probably more frequently due to intention on the part of the scribe)

Errors of Judgment

- Marginal notes in the exemplar could mistakenly be incorporated into the text.

How and why would they get into the exemplar?

Why would a scribe misunderstand?

Examples that seem to fit this:

John 5.3–5 in the KJV:
> "3 In these lay a great multitude of impotent folk, of blind, halt, withered, waiting for the moving of the water. 4 For an angel went down at a certain season into the pool, and troubled the water: whosoever then first after the troubling of the water stepped in was made whole of whatsoever disease he had. 5 And a certain man was there, which had an infirmity thirty and eight years."

John 3.13 in the KJV:
> "And no man hath ascended up to heaven, but he that came down from heaven, even the Son of man which is in heaven."

Errors due to Fatigue and Carelessness

• After six hours of copying a text, anyone would be prone to making nonsense changes to the text.

• It is possible to detect how much text a scribe copied in a day by noting when the greatest cluster of nonsense errors occur (often at the end of the day).

• It is difficult to distinguish these from errors due to carelessness in many MSS, unless one examines each MS fully.

Two examples from codex L (8th century):

1. John 1.1: Ἐν ἀρχῇ ἦν ὁ λόγος, καὶ ὁ λόγος ἦν πρὸς τὸν θεόν, καὶ ὁ θεὸς ἦν ὁ λόγος.

2. John 1.30: ὀπίσω μου ἔρχεται ἀήρ (aer)

The word is supposed to be ἀνήρ (aner)

To sum up:

Scribes made mistakes. Determining what sorts of mistakes they made takes skill and imagination. Knowing the basic categories of unintentional errors helps to eliminate possibilities for error. The fundamental principle of textual criticism is: Choose the reading that best explains the rise of the others.

ILLUSTRATIONS OF SCRIBAL CORRUPTIONS, PART 2: INTENTIONAL ERRORS

TEXTUAL CRITICISM

Two kinds of corruptions

1. Unintentional errors
2. Intentional changes

Intentional Errors:

Why would scribes intentionally change the text?

"Odd though it may seem, scribes who thought were more dangerous than those who wished to be faithful in copying what lay before them. Many of the alterations which may be classified as intentional were no doubt introduced in good faith by copyists who believed that they were correcting an error or infelicity of language which had previously crept into the sacred text and needed to be rectified."

Bruce Metzger, Text of the New Testament

Intentional Errors: Seven Categories

1. Spelling/Grammar Changes
2. Harmonizations
3. Correcting apparent discrepancies
4. Conflations
5. Explanatory glosses
6. Doctrinally motivated changes
7. Addition of enriching material

Spelling/Grammar Changes

- Tendency to change the grammar to conform to better Greek
- E.g., ἵνα + future indicative changed to aorist subjunctive:
- Rev 6.4: "so that people would butcher one another"
- The Byzantine scribes usually try to correct the grammar

Harmonizations

Four basic types:

1. Gospel parallels
2. OT quotations
3. Contextual parallels
4. Common expressions

Gospel parallels

- Luke 5.30:

  But the Pharisees and their experts in the law complained to his disciples, saying, "Why do you eat and drink with tax collectors and sinners?"

- Mark 2.16:

  When the experts in the law and the Pharisees saw that he was eating with sinners and tax collectors, they said to his disciples, "Why does he eat with tax collectors and sinners?"

Correcting apparent discrepancies

- Mark 1.2–3

  As it is written in Isaiah the prophet, "Look, I am sending my messenger ahead of you, who will prepare your way, the voice of one shouting in the wilderness, 'Prepare the way for the Lord, make his paths straight.'"

As it is written in the prophets...

Conflations

Conflation: combining two readings to make a new reading

- Byzantine MSS especially prone to conflate

- Luke 24.53: "They were continually in the temple blessing/praising/ blessing and praising God."

Explanatory glosses

- Eph 4.9: "Now what is the meaning of 'he ascended,' except that he also descended to the lower parts of the earth?"

- Most later MSS add "first" before "descended"

- 89 sequential verses in Mark 6–8 never mention Jesus by name or title...

Doctrinally motivated changes

Romans 8.1:

- Oldest witnesses: "There is therefore now no condemnation for those who are in Christ Jesus."

- Later witnesses add: "who do not walk according to the flesh"

- Even later witnesses add: "but who walk according to the Spirit"

Addition of enriching material

- Western text of Acts: 8.5% more material

Titles of some NT books:

- Revelation: 60 different titles

- Shortest: "The Revelation of John"

- Longest: "The Revelation of the all–glorious Evangelist, bosom–friend [of Jesus], virgin, beloved to Christ, John the theologian, son of Salome and Zebedee, but adopted son of Mary the Mother of God, and Son of Thunder" (codex 1775)

Summary

Scribes changed the text unintentionally (far more common) and intentionally. Most intentional changes were due to piety or desire for clarification A major criterion for determining the original wording therefore is: The harder reading is to be preferred.

SESSIONS #13 & #14
SOME FAMOUS MANUSCRIPTS: PAPYRI

TEXTUAL CRITICISM

NT Papyri in General

- Almost all discovered after 20th century began
- 127 total so far, all fragmentary
- Contain about half of NT
- Dates: II–VIII
- Within c. 125 years of NT, 43%+ of verses
- Importance is their date: earliest witnesses
- Generally confirm superiority of Alexandrian text

John Rylands Papyrus: P52
Chester Beatty Papyri: P45, P46, P47
Bodmer Papyri: P66, P75

P52

- Background: F. C. Baur and the Tübingen School
- 90 Years of Skepticism
- 1934: C. H. Roberts and his Discovery

The Discovery of P52

Text of P52

31–33:
the Jews, "For us it is not permitted to kill anyone," so that the word of
Jesus might be fulfilled, which he spoke signifying what kind of death
he was going to die. Entered thus again into the Praetorium Pilate and
he summoned Jesus and said to him, "Are you the king of the Jews?"

37–38:
A King I am. For this I have been born and [for this] I have come into
the world so that I would testify to the truth. Everyone who is of the
truth hears my voice." Said to him Pilate, "What is truth?" and this after
saying, again he went out unto the Jews and said to them, "I find not
one fault in him."

Chester Beatty Papyri: P45, P46, P47

- Chester Beatty, collector
- Purchase of MSS in Egypt
- Most housed at CBL
- 30 leaves of P46 at University of Michigan
- Published in 1930s
- Date: third century
- Matthew, John, Luke, Mark, Acts
- Oldest MS of Mark's Gospel
- 30 leaves of an original 112
- Text is a bit puzzling, 'improved' Alex?

P47

- Date: 3rd Century
- Revelation
- Oldest MS of Revelation
- Ten leaves
- Excellent text, one of the most important MSS of the Apocalypse

P46

- Date: c. AD 200
- Paul's letters + Hebrews
- Oldest MS of Paul
- 86 leaves of an original 104
- Single quire
- 2 Thessalonians, Philemon, Pastorals missing

P46: Ephesians 1

- Eph 1.1 in most translations: "...to the saints who are in Ephesus and are faithful"

- Eph 1.1 in B, P46: "...to the saints who are and are faithful"

How to explain this?

Bodmer Papyri: P66, P75

- Purchased by Martin Bodmer of Geneva
- Published in the 1950s and 1960s
- P66 has most of John, dated c. AD 175
- P75 has most of Luke and John, dated c. AD 200+

P66

- Did not contain the pericope adulterae
- Early, very important MS of John
- But scribe was more concerned with calligraphy than text

P75

- Did not contain the pericope adulterae
- Early, very important MS of Luke & John
- Scribe copied one letter at a time
- Faithful, private copy
- Closest ally: Codex Vaticanus
- Gift to Vatican in 2006

Luke 24, John 1 in P75
- Oldest MS with end of one Gospel and beginning of another on same page.

The side-by-side comparison of P66 & P75:
- Proof that professional scribes are not always the most faithful scribes

John 1.18

KJV: "No man hath seen God at any time; the only begotten Son, which is in the bosom of the Father, he hath declared him."

NET: "No one has ever seen God. The only one, himself God, who is in closest fellowship with the Father, has made God known."

Summary:

Papyri are extraordinarily important for text of NT

Compared to fuller, later MSS, they confirm text of "better" MSS

Codex Vaticanus: Ending of Luke, Beginning of John

SOME FAMOUS MANUSCRIPTS: MAJUSCULES

TEXTUAL CRITICISM

NT Majuscules in General

- Overall, the most important NT MSS

- Previously known as uncials

- Whole NT reproduced many times over

- Majuscule = capital letter MS on parchment

- Dates: III–X

- Designation: Latin letters, Greek letters, Hebrew letter OR

- arabic number with zero in front (01, 032)

- 322 majuscules

- Latest one discovered by CSNTM in 2004

Some Famous Manuscripts:

Majuscules
- Codex Vaticanus (B)
- Codex Bezae (D)
- Codex Alexandrinus (A)
- Codex Ephraemi Rescriptus (C)
- Codex Sinaiticus (‭א‬)
- Codex Washingtonianus (W)

Codex Vaticanus
- On earliest book list in Vatican Library—A.D. 1475
- Used by Erasmus indirectly and minimally
- Fourth century codex, most of the Bible
- Not well known until 19th century
- Best representative of Alexandrian text
- Text traced over in a later century
- Distigmai and textual variants

- Lacks Mark 16.9–20, John 7.53–8.11

Codex Bezae

- Donated to Cambridge University by Theodore Beza in 1581.
- Early fifth century
- Diglot
- a.k.a. Cantabrigiensis, Beza, D, 05
- Gospels and Acts
- Most eccentric NT MS: 'western' text.
- Copied as much as nine words at a time
- Very old text; western order of Gospels.
- Oldest MS with pericope adulterae.

Luke 6.4 agraphon in Bezae:
On the same day, when he saw someone working on the sabbath, he said to him, "Man, if you know what you are doing you are blessed; if you don't you are cursed and a transgressor of the Law."

Mark 1.40–41 in Bezae:
Now a leper came to him, asking him and saying, "If you are willing, you can heal me." And getting angry, [Jesus] stretched out his hand and touched him and said, "I am willing; be healed!"

Codex Alexandrinus

- Cyril Lucar, Patriarch of Constantinople, gave it to King Charles in 1627.
- Date: fifth century
- Byzantine in Gospels; Alexandrian for rest of NT
- Most important MS for Revelation

Section Titles for John

Codex Ephraemi Rescriptus

- Housed at the National Library of France
- Early fifth century
- Mixed text
- Palimpsest
- Codex Ephraemi Rescriptus
- Almost impossible to read undertext
- Constantine Tischendorf deciphered the text in 1840s—99%

Codex Sinaiticus

- Discovered by Tischendorf at Mt. Sinai in 1844
- He claimed the monks were burning its leaves
- Two more visits and he saw the NT (1859)
- Date: fourth century
- Alexandrian text
- Oldest complete NT
- Tischendorf's motive
- History of MS since 1859

Codex Washingtonianus

- Purchased by Charles Freer in 1906
- Date: late 4th/early 5th century
- a.k.a. Codex W (032)

- Western order of Gospels
- Most important Gospels MS in U.S.
- Patchwork text:
- Matthew, Luke 8.13–24.53: Byzantine
- Mark 1.1–5.30: Western
- Mark 5.31–16.20: Caesarean?
- Luke 1.1–8.12 & John 5.12–21.25: Alexandrian
- John 1.1–5.11: mixed
- Freer Logion between Mark 16.14 and 15:

And they excused themselves, saying, "This age of lawlessness and unbelief is under Satan, who does not allow the truth and power of God to prevail over the unclean things of the spirits. Therefore reveal thy righteousness now"—thus they spoke to Christ. And Christ replied to them, "The term of years of Satan's power has been fulfilled, but other terrible things draw near. And for those who have sinned I was delivered over to death, that they may inherit the spiritual and incorruptible glory of righteousness which is in heaven."

SESSIONS #17
RESOURCES FOR NEW TESTAMENT MANUSCRIPTS PT.1

TEXTUAL CRITICISM

Numerous Tools and Websites for NT Textual Criticism

The granddaddy of them all:

The Institute for New Testament Textual Research (Institut für neutestamentliche Textforschung or INTF)

INTF

- Founded in 1959 by Dr. Kurt Aland
- Part of the University of Muenster, Germany
- Purpose: complete investigation and publication of all NT MSS
- Productions: Nestle-Aland GNT, UBS GNT, ECM, Kurzgefasste

Liste, VMR (with University of Birmingham)

- Initial work: microfilms of 90% of all NT MSS

Brief Biography on Kurt Aland

- 1915–1994
- Professor in Halle, East Germany, after WWII
- Imprisoned in 1953, escaped with family in 1958
- Founded INTF in Muenster, West Germany, 1959
- Started working on the Nestle GNT, 22nd edition
- Took over the work; latest edition: NA28
- Loved his cigars!

INTF Productions

- Nestle-Aland GNT
- UBS GNT
- Editio critica maior: objective is to list every variant through first millennium
- Kurzgefasste Liste der griechischen Handschriften des Neuen Testaments (1963, 1994)
- Official catalog of GNT MSS
- Virtual Manuscript Room

Kurzgefasste Liste & Virtual Manuscript Room

- Both are now online tools
- egora.uni-muenster.de/intf/index_en.shtml gets you to both of them
- OR google "intf vmr wwu"

- Several search tools available on K-Liste
- Caveat lector: Internet access can be very slow
- Another site at INTF for accessing the K-Liste (earlier edition, different layout, much faster): intf.uni-muenster.de/vmr/NTVMR/Liste-Handschriften.php

The British Library: Codices Sinaiticus and Alexandrinus

Evangelical Textual Criticism Website
- Produced by scholars at Tyndale House, Cambridge
- evangelicaltextualcriticism.blogspot.com
- "a forum for people with knowledge of the Bible in its original languages to discuss its manuscripts and textual history from the perspective of historic evangelical theology"

Summary—Three Helpful Sites:
- INTF-VMR (in conjunction with University of Birmingham)
- British Library
- Evangelical Textual Criticism blogsite

SESSIONS #18

RESOURCES FOR NEW TESTAMENT MANUSCRIPTS PT.2

TEXTUAL CRITICISM

Center for the Study of New Testament Manuscripts (CSNTM)

What is CSNTM?

- Non-profit institute with 501(c)(3) status, founded 2002.

- Dedicated to digitally photographing all handwritten manuscripts of the New Testament.

- Use these manuscripts to get back to the original wording of the NT as much as is humanly possible.

How many manuscripts?

• As of September 2012: 5824 officially counted MSS (by the Institute for NT Textual Research [INTF], Muenster, Germany)

• Not all registered yet...

CSNTM

• Photography: 400+ NT MSS; 200,000+ pages photographed
• Collaboration: with INTF and other institutes

In the beginning, there was microfilm...

...and it was not good

Then came digital photography...

...and it was very good

CSNTM's priorities in photographing MSS

• Poor or politically unstable sites
• Where we have leads on uncatalogued MSS
• MSS known to be significant
• Every Greek NT MS

Some of the sites we've visited

• Ecumenical Patriarchate, Constantinople
• Monastery of St. John the Theologian, Patmos
• National Archives, Tirana, Albania
• University of Michigan, Ann Arbor
• Cambridge University
• Bavarian State Library, Munich
• Museum of Literature, Iasi, Romania

- Biblioteca Medicea Laurenziana, Florence

Albania

Florence: BML

Biblioteca Medicea Laurenziana

American School of Classics

University of Athens

Byzantine Historical Museum

Benaki Museum

Some manuscripts CSNTM has discovered

- Over 20,000 pages

- VII–XVIIIth century

CSNTM.ORG

Manuscript page

Rare Printed Books

Resources

Links

About the Center

CSNTM

Free for all, free for all time

SESSION #19

THE GREEK TEXT BEHIND THE KJV: ERASMUS & THE TEXTUS RECEPTUS

TEXTUAL CRITICISM

The KJV has been called "the single greatest monument to the English language."

One scholar claimed:

> "The supremacy of the King James is one of style, not of scholarship. The men who made it did not set out to manufacture a literary classic—classics are seldom made to order. Yet they did produce one: perhaps the only classic ever turned in by a committee…"

The linguist Mario Pei observed, "The King James Bible and Shakespeare together are responsible for well over half of all our language clichés and stock phrases."

H. L. Mencken, no friend of Christianity, declared that the KJV was "unquestionably the most beautiful book in the world."

Why such accolades?

It has rhythm, balance, dignity, and force of style that is unparalleled in any other translation.

But it's not perfect...

Two fundamental problems with the KJV:

1. Translation is dated

2. Textual basis is inferior

Behind the KJV...

Erasmus of Rotterdam

*   1466–1536

*   Humanist, Catholic scholar, very close to the ideals of the Reformation; best Greek scholar in western Europe in the 16th century.

Background

*   May 29, 1453: Turkish invasion of Byzantium

*   1454: movable type printing press invented by Johann Gutenberg

- March 1, 1516: Erasmus's text first printed NT to be published

- Complutensian Polyglot printed in Spain in 1514, but not published until 1522

- His Greek New Testament

- Five editions of the Greek NT

- First edition: Novum Instrumentum, 1 March 1516

- All were Greek-Latin diglots

- Basis: 7 MSS, none earlier than 11th century

His Greek New Testament

- Five editions of the Greek NT

- First edition: Novum Instrumentum, 1 March 1516

- All were Greek-Latin diglots

- Basis: 7 MSS, none earlier than 11th century

- First edition: Erasmus confessed that it was "thrown together rather than edited"

- called the most poorly edited book ever published

- Race against the Spaniards

Last leaf of the Apocalypse

- Revelation 22.16-21: Erasmus back-translated Latin into Greek, creating 17 textual variants not attested in any Greek manuscripts.

- Revelation 22.19: "And if any man shall take away from the words of the book of this prophecy, God shall take away his part out of the book of life, and out of the holy city, and from the things which are written in this book."

- Revelation 22.19: "And if any man shall take away from the words of the book of this prophecy, God shall take away his part out of the book of life..."

- All other Greek MSS have 'tree of life'

- Greek: ξύλου (xulou; tree) vs. βίβλου (biblou; book)

- Inner Latin error: libro (book) for ligno (tree)

The most notorious reading of the KJV:
Comma Johanneum (1 John 5.7–8)

1 John 5.7–8

- "For there are three that bear record in heaven, the Father, the Word, and the Holy Ghost: and these three are one. And there are three that bear witness in earth, the spirit, and the water, and the blood: and these three agree in one." (KJV)
- Most modern translations: "For there are three that testify, the Spirit and the water and the blood, and these three are in agreement."

The Comma Johanneum

First edition (1516):

- Trinitarian formula was not in Erasmus's text.
- 1 John 5.7 in Erasmus's first edition lacks the Trinitarian formula

Second edition: 1519 (Luther's Greek text):

- Outcry from ecclesiastical authorities that the Trinitarian formula in 1 John 5.7 (KJV) was not in his text.

- Erasmus's defense: no Greek MS support

- Somewhat disingenuous

- Other places he had no Greek witnesses, yet he wrote out the Greek for his text

•Scribe working at Oxford seems to have 'made to order' a complete NT manuscript, which eventually made its way to Erasmus.

Third edition (1522):

•Erasmus put the Trinitarian formula in his text at 1 John 5.7 because of ecclesiastical pressure (not because he promised to do so).

•Trinitarian formula at 1 John 5.7 is found only in nine late Greek manuscripts, four in the text and five in the margins. Erasmus's third edition was essentially used by the KJV translators.

Oldest MS:

•10th century, but the Trinitarian formula found in a much later marginal note

Oldest MS with Trinitarian formula in text:

•14th century

Summer 2010: Bavarian State Library

•Not found in any ancient versions except the Latin

•Not mentioned in the early church councils that affirmed the Trinity

Earliest certain evidence:

•Late fourth century, in the writings of Priscillian... the heretic

How did it get into the Bible?

Conclusions: Erasmus and the King James Bible

- Five editions (Erasmus)—>Stephanus (four editions) —>Beza (11 editions; 1589 and KJV)

- Inferior textual basis

- Only c. 5000 differences

- Essential doctrinal issues?

- Modern translations: 90% of the word of God?

- In spite of poor textual basis, KJV unmatched in literary quality

SESSIONS #20 & #21

THE TEXTUS RECEPTUS AND THE DOCTRINE OF PRESERVATION

TEXTUAL CRITICISM

Defining our Terms

- Textus Receptus: Essentially any Greek NT that is essentially derived from Erasmus's text

- Including all five of Erasmus's editions

- All four of Stephanus's editions

- All eleven of Beza's editions

- The editions of the Elzevirs (1633 first called textus receptus)

- More technically, the 1550 Stephanus text (3rd edition), which is also virtually identical with the 1825 and 1873 Oxford TR (the latter edited by   F. H. A. Scrivener)

- Defining our terms

- Doctrine of Preservation:
the doctrine that God has preserved scripture down to the very words

- Corollary of preservation for TR /MT advocates:

inspiration—>preservation—>accessibility—>majority

Select Statements from TR/MT Advocates

Jasper James Ray, God Wrote Only One Bible:

- "The TEXTUS RECEPTUS . . . is God's sure foundation on which to rest our eternal salvation" (p. 32)

- "It is impossible to be saved without 'FAITH,' and perfect-saving-faith can only be produced by the 'ONE' Bible God wrote, and that we find only in translations which agree with the Greek Textus Receptus refused by Westcott and Hort" (p. 122)

- "The Bible God wrote has been providentially preserved for us in the Greek Textus Receptus, from which the King James Bible was translated in 1611." (p. 106)

- "The writing of the Word of God by inspiration is no greater miracle than the miracle of its preservation in the Textus Receptus." (p. 104)

David Otis Fuller, Counterfeit or Genuine?

- He calls modern translations "bastard bibles" (p. 10)

- "born-again Christians in this twentieth century are facing the most malicious and vicious attack upon God's inspired Holy Word since the Garden of Eden. And this attack began in its modern form in the publication of the Revised Version of the Scriptures in 1881 in England" (p. 9).

David Otis Fuller, Which Bible? (5th edition):

- "Naturalistic New Testament critics seem to last to have reached the end of the trail. Westcott and Hort's broad highway, which appeared to lead so quickly and smoothly to the original New Testament text, has dwindled down to a narrow foot path and terminated finally in a thicket of trees. For those who have followed it, there is only one thing to do, and that is to go back and begin the journey all over again from the consistently Christian starting point; namely, the divine inspiration and providential preservation of Scripture." (pp. 8–9)

Wilbur Pickering, Identity of the New Testament Text:

- "Aleph and B have lied"; "Aleph is clearly a bigger liar than B" (p. 126).

- All the ancient manuscripts on which modern critical text are based are "convicted liars all" (p. 135).

- "the doctrine of Divine Preservation of the New Testament Text depends upon the interpretation of the evidence which recognizes the Traditional Text to be the continuation of the autographa" (p. 91).

Summing up

- Inspiration implies preservation, which implies accessibility, which implies majority.

- Or conversely, if it's in the majority of MSS (or printed NTs), it is thus accessible; if accessible, it's because it's been preserved for all to read; if it's been preserved for all, then it's inspired.

Critique

1. Question-begging approach

2. Faulty assumptions

3. Non-biblical doctrinal basis

Question-begging approach

What do you count?

When do you count?

Where do you count?

Faulty Assumptions

Preservation a necessary corollary of inspiration

- Logic: all MSS, group of MSS, one MS

- TR: Erasmus just as inspired as apostles

Preservation must be through "majority rule"

- Where taught in Bible?

- 2 Kings 22.8–13: only one copy of the Law

- Biblically, usually the remnant is right/holy/true against the majority

- Historically: Discovery of Sinaiticus, etc.

Public accessibility of a pure text theologically necessary

- TR not published till 1516

- 30 different editions of TR: which is the pure text?

- MT was not published until 1982; at least four different versions now

- No translations of MT yet made

Certainty identical with truth

- Must be relative: which TR? which MT? which KJV?

- Many religious groups have absolute certainty

- Can only be claimed since printing press

- What doctrines are at stake?

- Waffling on what is 'absolute'

- Pursuit of certainty vs. pursuit of truth

Non-biblical doctrinal basis

A Marcionite view of the text: the doctrine doesn't work for the OT

- "God must do more than merely preserve the inspired original New Testament text. He must preserve it in a public way . . . through the continuous usage of His Church" (E.F. Hills, The King James Version Defended! [p. 66])

- What about the Old Testament? Hebrew Bible preserved by Christians?

A Marcionite view of the text: the doctrine doesn't work for the OT

- Several readings found only in the versions are authentic

- Several authentic readings not discovered until DSS

- Some places in OT are corrupt in all MSS

- 2 Chron 36.9 vs. 2 Kings 24.8: Jehoiakim 8 or 18?

- 2 Chron 22.2 vs. 2 Kings 8.26: Ahaziah 22 or 42?

This doctrine not taught in the Bible

- Metzger: "I think it's the wisest course of action to embrace only those doctrines that we can find in scripture"

- Not a doctrine of the ancient church: 1646, 1675

- Non-biblical doctrinal basis

- Proof-texts: Ps 119.89, Isa 40:8, Matt 5:18, Matt 24.35

- Ps 119.89: "Your word, O Lord, is forever settled in heaven"

- Isa 40.8: "The grass withers, the flower fades, but the word of our God stands forever" (NET: "the decree of our God is forever reliable")

- Matt 5.18: "Till heaven and earth pass, one jot or one tittle shall in no wise pass from the law, till all be fulfilled" (KJV)

- Non-biblical doctrinal basis

- Matt 24.35: "Heaven and earth will pass away, but my words will never pass away"

Conclusion

There is no biblical, exegetical, or empirical basis to argue for the doctrine of preservation to argue for this doctrine is bibliologically schizophrenic and thus Marcionite

What can we say about preservation then?

THE HISTORY OF NT TC SINCE THE TEXTUS RECEPTUS

TEXTUAL CRITICISM

Overview of Textus Receptus

- Erasmus's five editions (1516–1535)

- Complutensian Polyglot (1514)

- Stephanus's four editions (1546–1551)

- Beza's eleven editions (1564–1604)

- The Elzevirs's two editions (1624, 1633)

- Dozens of others

Since the Textus Receptus

Variant readings collected:

- Brian Walton, London Polyglot (1657)—first systematic collection of variant readings

- John Mill, Novum Testamentum (1707): 2 volumes, 30,000 variants (100 MSS + versions and fathers)

  o   Caused alarm among Protestants, glee among Catholics
  o   Ably defended by Richard Bentley (1713)

- Johann Albrecht Bengel (1687–1752):

  o   Alexandrian and Byzantine families
  o   Canon of harder reading
  o   Rating system: α, β, γ, δ, ε
  o   articulated orthodoxy of the variants

Principles articulated:

- J. J. Griesbach (1745–1812)

  o   Canon of shorter reading
  o   Fifteen canons of internal evidence
  o   interplay between external and internal evidence
  o   recognized three text-types: Alexandrian, Western, Byzantine
  o   Not orthodox...

First printed text to break completely from the Textus Receptus:

- Karl Lachmann (1793–1851)

    o   No printed texts used
    o   No minuscules used
    o   Excellent principles employed
    o   Only majuscules, versions, fathers

- Constantin von Tischendorf (1815–1874)

    o   Motivated by threat of F. C. Baur; committed to evangelical faith
    o   Discovered and published numerous MSS of NT, LXX, other ancient literature
    o   Deciphered Ephraemi Rescriptus
    o   Discovered Sinaiticus
    o   Published eight editions of GNT; last included most complete apparatus up to that time, still valuable today
    o   Regarded as best NT textual critic of all time

- Samuel Prideaux Tregelles (1813–1875)

    o   Best Englishman at amassing data for a critical text
    o   Plymouth Brethren, evangelical, posttribulational
    o   Learned Greek, Hebrew, Aramaic, and Latin while employed at an iron works
    o   Produced a superb two-volume NT with extensive apparatus (1857–1872), as an act of worship to the triune God
    o   If Tischendorf had not lived, Tregelles might well be considered the best NT textual critic of all time

B. F. Westcott and F. J. A. Hort's three major accomplishments:

1. Clearest articulation of method to date that has largely stood the test of time

2. Overthrew the Textus Receptus

3. Produced The New Testament in the Original Greek (1881); Introduction [and] Appendix (1882)

o 28 years of labor

o Virtually all GNTs today take their starting point from WH

o Westcott orthodox, Hort probably not

20th Century Scholars

- Caspar Rene Gregory (1846–1917)

- Günther Zuntz, Text of the Epistles (1953)

- E. C. Colwell (1901–1974)

- Kurt (1915–94) and Barbara Aland (INTF)

- Bruce M. Metzger (1914–2007)

- Harry Sturz

- Gordon D. Fee

TISCHENDORF AND THE DISCOVERY OF CODEX SINAITICUS

TEXTUAL CRITICISM

St. Catherine's Monastery

Patent of Muhammed

This is a message from Muhammad ibn Abdullah, as a covenant to those who adopt Christianity, near and far, we are with them.

Verily I, the servants, the helpers, and my followers defend them, because Christians are my citizens; and by Allah! I hold out against anything that displeases them.

No compulsion is to be on them.

Neither are their judges to be removed from their jobs nor their monks from their monasteries.

No one is to destroy a house of their religion, to damage it, or to carry anything from it to the Muslims' houses.

In Tischendorf's own words:

"It was in April, 1844, that I embarked at Leghorn for Egypt. The desire which I felt to discover some precious remains of any manuscripts, more especially Biblical, of a date which would carry us back to the early times of Christianity, was realized beyond my expectations. It was at the foot of Mount Sinai, in the Convent of St. Catherine, that I discovered the pearl of all my researches. In visiting the library of the monastery, in the month of May, 1844, I perceived in the middle of the great hall a large and wide basket full of old parchments; and the librarian, who was a man of information, told me that two heaps of papers like these, mouldered by time, had been already committed to the flames. What was my surprise to find amid this heap of papers [was] a considerable number of sheets of a copy of the Old Testament in Greek, which seemed to me to be one of the most ancient that I had ever seen."

Tischendorf had three visits to St. Catherine's:

1. 1854
2. 1853
3. 1859

The 1859 visit was under sponsorship of the Tsar of Russia, Alexander II. On the last day of this visit, Feb 4, the steward of the monastery showed him a codex:

> "He took down from the corner of the room a bulky kind of volume, wrapped up in a red cloth, and laid it before me. I unrolled the cover, and discovered, to my great surprise, not only those very fragments which, fifteen years before, I had taken out of the basket, but also other parts of the Old Testament, the New Testament complete, and, in addition, the Epistle of Barnabas and a part of the Pastor of Hermas. Full of joy, which this time I had the self-command to conceal from the steward and the rest of the community, I asked, as if in a careless way, for permission to take the manuscript into my sleeping chamber to look over it more at leisure. ... I knew that I held in my hand the most precious Biblical treasure in existence—a document whose age and importance exceeded that of all the manuscripts which I had ever examined during twenty years' study of the subject."

Sinaiticus Today

Two Leaves of Sinaiticus found at Mt. Sinai in 1975

Text of Tischendorf's note:

> "I, the undersigned, Constantin Tischendorf, attest that the Holy Confraternity of Mount Sinai has delivered to me as a loan an ancient manuscript of both Testaments, being the property of the aforesaid monastery and containing 346 leaves and a small fragment. These I shall take with me to St. Petersburg in order that I may collate the copy previously made by me with the original at the time of publication of the manuscript.... This manuscript I promise to return, undamaged and in a good state of preservation, to the Holy Confraternity of Sinai at its earliest request."

WESTCOTT-HORT & THE DETHRONING OF THE TEXTUS RECEPTUS

TEXTUAL CRITICISM

Who were Westcott and Hort?

Brooke Foss Westcott

- 1825–1901

- Trained at Cambridge University in classical Greek and Latin

- Age 24: began teaching at Cambridge

- Voluminous writer: Gospels, commentaries, deity of Christ, resurrection, canon, English Bible, Greek NT

- 1870: Regius Professor of Divinity at Cambridge

Fenton John Anthony Hort

- 1828–1892

- Born in Dublin

- Hulsean Professor of Divinity, then Lady Margaret Professor of Divinity, Cambridge

- Exacting scholar, but prone to leave scholarly works unfinished

- 1881–82: He and Westcott published The New Testament in the Original Greek (2 vols.)

Westcott and Hort & their Greek text (1881)

WH's NT: Eye of the Storm

- Strong reaction by Dean Burgon and later, by KJV Only advocates, against Westcott and Hort

- Beginning with Burgon, ad hominem was used

- 20th century followers of Burgon more vicious, claiming:

  o   Westcott denied the deity of Christ
  o   Westcott denied the resurrection of Christ
  o   Hort denied all sorts of cardinal doctrines
  o   WH were involved in occult

- Extreme example: G. A. Riplinger, New Age Bible Versions (1993)

  o   1000s of copies sold; hundreds of churches abandoned modern translations

  o   Confuses B.F. Westcott with W.W. Westcott: the latter was indeed involved in the occult

In the magazine Borderland (1893), a magazine dedicated to the occult, Westcott wrote a letter to the editor:

> "Many years ago I had occasion to investigate spiritualistic phenomena with some care, and I came to a clear conclusion, which I feel bound to express in answer to your circular. It appears to me that in this, as in all spiritual questions, Holy Scripture is our supreme guide. I observe, then, that while spiritual [i.e., spiritist] ministries are constantly recorded in the Bible, there is not the faintest encouragement to seek them. The case, indeed, is far otherwise. I cannot, therefore, but regard every voluntary approach to beings such as those who are supposed to hold communication with men through mediums as unlawful and perilous. I find in the fact of the Incarnation all that man (so far as I can see) requires for life and hope."

What Westcott believed about the resurrection:

> "Indeed taking all the evidence together, it is not too much to say that there is no single historic incident better or more variously supported than the Resurrection of Christ. Nothing but the antecedent assumption that it must be false could have suggested the idea of deficiency in the proof of it."

What Westcott believed about the deity of Christ:

- "His work was to take away sins: He Himself was sinless"

- "The exalted king [Christ], who is truly man, is also above all finite beings"
- "He [Christ] is at once Creator and Heir of all things"

- "Christ the Incarnate Word is the perfect revelation of the Father: as God, He reveals God."

What about Hort?

- More difficult to determine (published far less than Westcott), but probably not as orthodox as Westcott.

- Ironically: considered a 'papist' by some KJV Only folks!

Relevance?

Westcott-Hort's work

- 28 years of incessant labor

- Two volumes: The New Testament in the Original Greek (1881); Introduction [and] Appendix (1882)

- Immediately claimed as a major advance in understanding the transmission of the NT

- Three basic arguments against TR and Byzantine text:

    1. No distinctive Byzantine readings in ante-Nicene Fathers: thus, LATE

    2. Byzantine readings not supported by intrinsic evidence (author) or transcriptional evidence (scribe): thus, INFERIOR

    3. Only the Byzantine text-form conflates; Alexandrian & Western always the 'legs' that the Byzantine conflation stands on; never is the Byzantine one of the legs: thus, SECONDARY

        1. No distinctive Byzantine readings in ante-Nicene fathers:

            - Response: (1) Yes there are (Burgon); (2) No there are not, but too few literary remains of ante-Nicene Byzantine fathers (Sturz)

        2. Byzantine readings not supported by intrinsic evidence (author) or transcriptional evidence (scribe)

            - Response: (1) Internal evidence too subjective to count; (2) Yes they are

            - Phil 1.14

            - "and most of the brothers and sisters, having confidence in the Lord because of my imprisonment, now more than ever dare to speak the word fearlessly."

            - A B D ℵ add 'of God' to 'the word'

- F G (Western MSS) add 'of the Lord' to 'the word'

- Byz 1739 P46 add nothing

3. Only the Byzantine text-form conflates; Alexandrian & Western always the 'legs' that the Byzantine conflation stands on; never is the Byzantine one of the legs

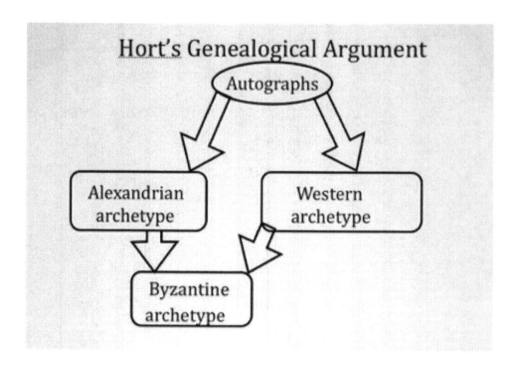

Illustration: Luke 24.53
"in the temple, {blessing/praising/blessing and praising} God"

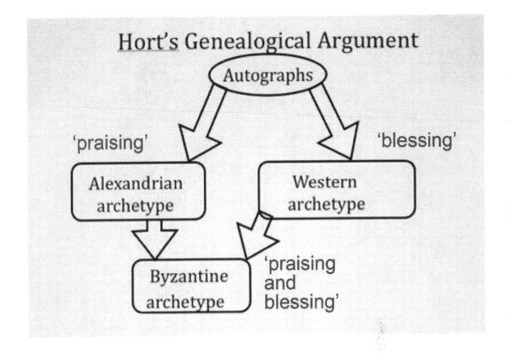

Luke 9.10: "they withdrew by themselves to a...

"   town called Bethsaida" (Alex)
"deserted place   called Bethsaida" (West)
"deserted place of a town called Bethsaida" (Byz)

It's virtually impossible for the Alexandrian & Western text-forms to accidentally drop out part of the reading. Greek:

πολιν   καλουμενην Βηθσαιδα (Alex)
τοπον ερημον   καλουμενον Βηθσαιδα (West)
τοπον ερημον πολεως καλουμενης Βηθσαιδαν (Byz)

---

                polIN   kaloumenen   Bethsaida (Alex)
topon eremon   kaloumenON   Bethsaida (West)
topon eremon polEOS kaloumeneS   BethsaidaN (Byz)

Summary

Westcott & Hort argued that the Byzantine text was:

1.   Late (no ante-Nicene distinctive Byzantine readings)

2.   Inferior (no good readings internally)

3.   Secondary (always recipient of other readings to make a conflate reading)

SESSION #26

REASONED ECLECTICISM PART1: INTRODUCTION, IN-TERNAL EVIDENCE

TEXTUAL CRITICISM

Introduction:

Competing Views

Some definitions:

Internal evidence:
- what the biblical author was likely to have written (intrinsic probability);

- what the scribes were likely to have copied (transcriptional probability)

External evidence:
- focus on material—manuscripts, versions, fathers

School	Rigorous Eclecticism	Reasoned Eclecticism	Majority Text View
Emphasis	Internal priority	Roughly equal emphasis on internal and external	External priority
Advocates	G. D. Kilpatrick, J. K. Elliott	Bruce Metzger, Gordon Fee, Michael Holmes, and most textual critics	Zane Hodges, Maurice Robinson, only conservatives

Problems with Rigorous Eclecticism

- (Virtually) exclusive focus on internal evidence, especially intrinsic probability: in most cases, the most subjective aspect of textual criticism

- Just because all MSS are corrupt doesn't mean that they are equally so

- History gets short shrift

- Textual apparatus becomes little more than a pool of variants from which to choose the original reading

Problems with Majority Text Theory

- Focus on external evidence is selective: Just Greek MSS are considered

- When to count? Byzantine text-form did not become majority until the 9th century

- No Byzantine MSS, versions, or fathers before 4th century

- Only conservatives, but most conservatives hold to reasoned eclecticism

- See Hort's critique of Byzantine text

Reasoned Eclecticism

- Not always even-handed in its application (frequently strong bias against Byzantine and Western text)

- Does not fully integrate church history into transmission of NT text

- BUT: in spite of the failings in its execution, it is the most balanced approach, weighing internal and external evidence evenly

Internal Evidence

Three principles:

- The guiding principle of internal evidence (and of all evidence): choose the reading that best explains the rise of the others.

Two important sub-principles:

1. The harder reading is to be preferred

2. The shorter reading is to be preferred

The harder reading is to be preferred:

- ambiguous, cumbersome, awkward, wording; rarer words, unusual grammar, wording that could be perceived as a discrepancy

- *Why is this preferred?*

  Scribes were prone to smooth out the text, make it clearer, explain things.

- *When is the harder reading not to be preferred?*

Harder reading analogy

Tolkien's Lord of the Rings (Strider meets the hobbits at the Prancing Pony Inn, and announces that he is Aragorn):

There was a long silence. At last Frodo spoke with hesitation, "I believed that you were a friend before the letter came," he said, "or at least I wished to. You have frightened me several times tonight, but never in the way that servants of the Enemy would, or so I imagine. I think one of his spies would—well, seem fairer and feel fouler, if you understand."

Illustrations of harder readings:

- Matthew 27.16–17

At that time they had in custody a notorious prisoner named Jesus Barabbas. 17 So after they had assembled, Pilate said to them,

"Whom do you want me to release for you, Jesus Barabbas or Jesus who is called the Christ?" [NET]

Most MSS omit 'Jesus' before Barabbas both times.

- *Which is the harder reading?*

- Any page in Aland's Synopsis of the Four Gospels reveals harmonizations in various MSS

- Mark 6:31–8:26: 'he' vs. 'Jesus' (vv. 6.34, 7.27, 8.1, 8.17)

- Mark 1.2: "in Isaiah the prophet" vs. "in the prophets"

- Titles of Gospels (though not part of the original text): "Gospel according to _____" vs. "according to _____" P66 & P75 vs. Sinaiticus (01) and Vaticanus (03)

Internal evidence

The shorter reading is to be preferred:

- like a rolling snow ball, foreign material was added to the NT over time. Not as much we might think, however.

- Why is this preferred? Scribes were prone to explain things, add titles, phrases, descriptors, etc.

- When is the shorter reading not to be preferred?

Shorter Reading Analogy

Illustrations of shorter readings:

- Once again, Mark 6:31–8:26: 'he' vs. 'Jesus' (vv. 6.34, 7.27, 8.1, 8.17)

- Titles of Gospels (though not part of the original text): "Gospel according to _____" vs. "according to _____" P66 & P75 vs. Sinaiticus (01) and Vaticanus (03)

- BUT: Matt 27.16–17: Jesus Barabbas

Internal Evidence

- Two divisions:

  1. Transcriptional probability: Which variants did the scribes most likely create?

  2. Intrinsic probability: What did the biblical author most likely write?

Internal Evidence:

Transcriptional Probability

- Two elements:

  1. Unintentional errors

2.   Intentional errors

Internal Evidence:

Intrinsic Probability

- Two key elements, one general principle:

    1.   Context

    2.   Style

- Principle: The more material, the more objective the conclusions

Context:

- John 14.17:

"The Spirit of truth, whom the world cannot accept, because it does not see him or know him. But you know him, because he resides with you and {will be/is} in you."

- Cf. John 6.63:

"Now he said this about the Spirit, whom those who believed in him were going to receive, for the Spirit had not yet been given, because Jesus was not yet glorified."

- Cf. also John 20.22; Acts 1.8; Acts 2.4

Style:

- Mark 16:9–20

Language is quite unlike the rest of Mark. Coupled with strong external testimony, the evidence is overwhelming that it's not authentic.

Summary

Three broad principles:

1. choose the reading with explanatory power

2. harder reading

3. shorter reading

Two divisions:

1. Transcriptional evidence

2. Intrinsic evidence

Relation of internal to external evidence:

SESSION #27
REASONED ECLECTICISM PART 2: EXTERNAL EVIDENCE

TEXTUAL CRITICISM

Internal vs. External

- All internal evidence is somewhat subjective

- All manuscripts are somewhat corrupt

- Scholars have to work through both sides of the issue

- Reasoned eclecticism is the only approach that considers both components evenly (or should!)

External Evidence

- What is a text-type?

The largest group of manuscripts with a common ancestor (other than the original text)

- Illustration: NKJV vs. NASB

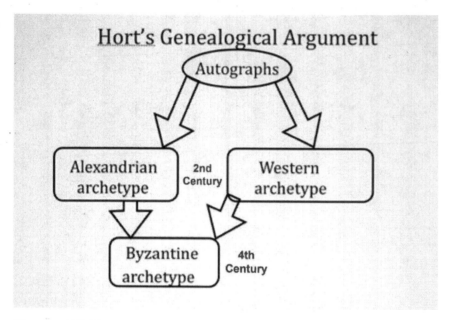

External Evidence

Three aspects:

1. Date and character
2. Genealogical solidarity
3. Geographical distribution

Date and Character of MSS:

- The closer in time to the original, the better the manuscript.

- Manuscripts from a faithful line of copying are to be preferred.

- Manuscripts obviously done carefully are to be preferred.

Genealogical Solidarity:

- If the older and better manuscripts of a particular text-type agree, it is more likely that they represent the wording of their 'local original.'

- If virtually all the MSS of a text-type agree, they almost surely represent the reading of their local original.

Geographical Distribution:

- The more widespread a textual variant is, the more likely it reflects the wording of the original.

This is especially true in the earlier centuries of copying.

Relation of Genealogical Solidarity to Geographical Distribution

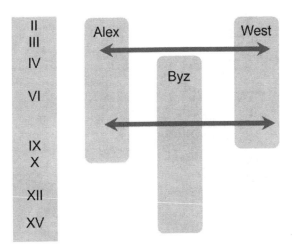

Illustrations

- Mark 1.2: "in Isaiah the prophet" vs. "in the prophets"

    o   "in Isaiah the prophet"—best Alexandrian & Western witnesses

    o   "in the prophets"—almost all Byzantine MSS

- Mark 1.1: "The beginning of the gospel of Jesus Christ, the Son of God."

    o   Alexandrian witnesses split: Sinaiticus lacks phrase, Vaticanus & others have it.

    o   Western & Byzantine solid for the phrase

- Titles of Gospels (though not part of the original text): "Gospel according to _____" vs. "according to _____"

    o   Best Alexandrian MSS lack "Gospel" (Sinaiticus (א) & Vaticanus (B)

    o   All other witnesses have "Gospel" if they have the title at all.

- John 14.17:
    o   "The Spirit of truth, whom the world cannot accept, be cause it does not see him or know him. But you know him, because he resides with you and {will be/is} in you."
    o   P66, B, D, W read: "is"
    o   Virtually all others read "will be"
    o   Alexandrian is split, but Byzantine and Western are solid.
    o   How to solve this? Internal evidence needs to have a say.

Conclusion

- External evidence has to do with the material witnesses—that is, the MSS, versions, and fathers.

- Millions of man-hours have been expended on the examination of these witnesses in the last 300+ years.

- We have learned that witnesses must be weighed, not counted.

- The examination of date & character, genealogical solidarity, and geographical distribution is key to understanding the value of the witnesses.

- Using internal and external evidence in combination requires finesse and imagination.

REASONED ECLECTICISM PART 3: PUTTING IT ALL TOGETHER

TEXTUAL CRITICISM

Basic Principle of Textual Criticism:

Choose the reading that best explains the rise of the others.

Basic approach:

- Examine internal evidence first; if a variant is predictable, then some scribe somewhere was probably tempted to create it.

- Give a letter grade to the preferred reading from the internal examination.

- Examine the external evidence, without regard for your tentative conclusion from internal considerations.

- Give a letter grade to the preferred reading from the external examination

Combine the two grades, keeping in mind the basic principle.

Illustrations

I have chosen one easy and three very difficult problems to illustrate the whole process.

- Revelation 1.4: "From John, to the seven churches that are in the province of Asia: Grace and peace to you from 'he who is,' and who was, and who is still to come, and from the seven spirits who are before his throne" [NET]

    o   Variant: 'from God who is'

Revelation 1.4: "he who is" vs. "God who is"

Internal evidence:

- Transcriptional probability: grammatical error in 'he who is'; significantly softened with 'God who is'
- Intrinsic probability: we will address this at the end...
- Grade: A for 'he who is'

External evidence:

- No 'western' text for Revelation, but almost all Latin witnesses have 'he who is'
- Alexandrians solid for 'he who is'
- Byzantines split, but most have 'God who is'
- Grade: A for 'he who is'

- Revelation 1.4: "he who is" vs. "God who is"

    o Intrinsic probability:
    o Revelation 1.3:
    "Blessed is the one who reads the words of this prophecy, and blessed are those who keep the things written in it"
    o Historical situation: John exiled on Patmos
    o Exodus 3.14: "God said to Moses, 'I AM that I AM.'"

- Revelation 1.4: "he who is" vs. "God who is"

    o Intrinsic probability:
    - Analogy: Preamble to the Constitution: "We the people of the United States..."
    - No quotation marks in Greek
    - 250+ quotations of OT in Revelation...

Mark 1.1: "The beginning of the gospel of Jesus Christ, the Son of God."

Internal evidence:

- Transcriptional: shorter, harder reading is to be preferred
- Intrinsic: Mark's style and context suggest 'the Son of God' is authentic.

Mark 1.1: "The beginning of the gospel of Jesus Christ, the Son of God."

- Mark 1.1 served as title to the book
- 'Son of God' comes at key places in Gospel:
  - 1.11: "you are my beloved Son"
  - 3.11: demons declare: "you are the Son of God"
  - 9.11: "This is my beloved Son"

- Mark 1.1: "The beginning of the gospel of Jesus Christ, the Son of God."
  - o Inclusion: "Now when the centurion, who stood in front of him, saw how he died, he said, 'Truly this man was God's Son!'" [Mark 15.39, NET]

- Mark 1.1: "The beginning of the gospel of Jesus Christ, the Son of God."
  - o Alexandrian witnesses split: Sinaiticus lacks phrase, Vaticanus & others have it.
  - o Western & Byzantine solid for the phrase

- Mark 1.1: "The beginning of the gospel of Jesus Christ, the Son of God."
  - o How to explain ℵ's reading: first corrector, nomina sacra and genitive strings
    - First corrector adds "the Son of God"

- Mark 1.1: "The beginning of the gospel of Jesus Christ, the Son of God."
  - o nomina sacra: contracted sacred names
  - o genitive strings: words with similar endings
  - o Combined in Mark 1.1:
    - Ἀρχὴ τοῦ εὐαγγελίου Ἰησου Χριστοῦ. (five words in a row ending in upsilon)
    - Does ℵ elsewhere skip words in such strings? Yes: TEN times! E.g., Acts 28.31; Col 2.2; Heb 12.2; Rev 12.14; 15.7;

22.1.

- Mark 1.1: "The beginning of the gospel of Jesus Christ, the Son of God."
  - o   Conclusion: Internal and external evidence combined suggest that 'the Son of God' is authentic in Mark 1.1.
  - o   "if [the title] was not part of the original superscription it should have been, and the scribe who first added it was Markan in purpose if not in name." —Norman Perrin

John 14.17: "he resides with you and will be in you"

- Transcriptional probability: harder reading is 'is'
- Intrinsic probability: very strong that 'will be' instead of 'is' is authentic.
  - o   Cf. John 6.63: "Now he said this about the Spirit, whom those who believed in him were going to receive, for the Spirit had not yet been given, because Jesus was not yet glorified."
  - o   Cf. also John 20.22; Acts 1.8; Acts 2.4
- Grade: B for 'will be'

John 14.17: "he resides with you and will be in you"

- External evidence: more difficult to assess:
  - o   P66* B D* W read "is"
  - o   Virtually all other witnesses read "will be" (including ℵ, P75, P66c, and Dc)
  - o   But P66 and B are excellent Alexandrian witnesses; D is the best Western witness
  - o   Grade slightly in favor of 'will be': D

John 14.17: "he resides with you and will be in you"

- Although external evidence is not compelling, the intrinsic evidence is: 'will be' is almost surely what John wrote.
- At bottom, choosing the reading that best explains the rise of the other(s) seems to suggest that 'will be' is authentic.

Reasoned Eclecticism:

Illustrations

- Matthew 27.16–17 (Internal Evidence)

  o   "Jesus Barabbas" vs. "Barabbas"
  o   No unintentional reason for adding "Jesus" before "Barabbas" can be found. (The last time "Jesus" is mentioned is in v. 11.)
  o   Intentional error? Dropping of 'Jesus'

- Matthew 27.16–17 (Internal evidence)

  o   Intrinsic probability: The Greek may give a telltale sign that Matthew wrote "Jesus Barabbas":
  o   v. 17: "Whom do you want me to release for you, Jesus the Barabbas or Jesus the one who is called the Christ?"
  o   'the' with 'Barabbas' and 'Christ' seems to distinguish two different men, both named Jesus.
  o   Internally, the addition of 'Jesus' rates a solid A.

- Matthew 27.16–17 (External evidence)

  o   "Jesus Barabbas" vs. "Barabbas"
  o   Most MSS omit 'Jesus' before Barabbas both times, including virtually all Alex, West, & Byz.

- o   Only a few MSS have "Jesus."
- o   Externally, the omission rates a solid A.

- Matthew 27.16–17

  - o   Additional factors: Origen (early third century): "in the whole range of the scriptures we know that no one who is a sinner [is called] Jesus."
    - •   Origen's statement reveals that he knew of the 'Jesus' reading in his day, even though our earliest MSS now are from the 9th century.

- Matthew 27.16–17

  - o   Additional factors: in about 20 late MSS, a marginal note: "In many ancient copies which I have met with I found Barabbas himself likewise called 'Jesus'..."
  - o   This note was attributed to various church fathers, including Chrysostom and Origen.

- Matthew 27.16–17

  - o   This is one of the more difficult problems in the NT to solve.
  - o   BUT: the fundamental principle gives the nod to the longer reading: "Jesus Barabbas."
  - o   Both because of the possibility of accidentally dropping out the name of Jesus after 'you', and especially the pious motive which Origen articulates, argues that Matthew originally wrote "Jesus Barabbas" in both v. 16 and v. 17.

SOME FAMOUS TEXTUAL PROBLEMS

TEXTUAL CRITICISM

Mark 1:41

(40) Now a leper came to him and fell to his knees, asking for help. "If you are willing, you can make me clean," he said.

o   Reading 1: (41) Moved with compassion, Jesus stretched out his hand and touched him, saying, "I am willing. Be clean!" [NET]

o   Reading 2: (41) Becoming indignant, Jesus stretched out his hand and touched him saying, "I am willing. Be clean!"

Mark 1.41: Internal Evidence

Transcriptional probability

- Unintentional error: splangchnistheis   orgistheis

- Intentional change: Harder reading: orgistheis (becoming indignant)

Harder reading: orgistheis (becoming indignant)

- Mark was first Gospel, used by Matthew and Luke

- Synoptic parallels: Matthew & Luke have neither word

- Matthew and Luke are prone to soften Mark's rough-hewn Jesus, especially by deleting words:

    o   Mark 3.5: Jesus speaks 'with anger' ('with anger' absent in Matt 12.13 & Luke 6.10

    o   Mark 10.14: Jesus 'was indignant' ('was indignant' absent from Matt 19.14 & Luke 16.18)

    o   Mark 1.12: the Spirit drove Jesus into the wilderness (Matt 4.1 & Luke 4.1: the Spirit led [up] Jesus into the wilderness)

    o   Mark 2.26: 'when Abiathar was high priest' (absent in Matt 12.4 & Luke 6.4)

Intrinsic probability: style

- Two other times Mark says Jesus is angry (3.5, 10.14)

- Mark is often amiguous; here, why Jesus would be angry

Internal evidence: solid A for 'becoming angry'

Mark 1.41: External Evidence

- Date and character:

  o   D a ff2 r1* Ephrem's commentary on Tatian's Diatessaron: 'becoming angry'

  o   The rest of the witnesses: 'moved with compassion'

- Genealogical solidarity:

  o   Alexandrian and Byzantine: solidly behind the compassionate Jesus

  o   Western: strongly in support of the angry Jesus

- Geographical distribution:

  o   'moved with compassion' widespread
  o   'becoming angry' largely isolated to Western text

External evidence: solid A for 'moved with compassion'

Mark 1.41: Conclusion

Choose the reading that best explains the rise of the other.

- Synoptic parallels show that Mark's Jesus was angry

- Scribes would be prone to change text to a compassionate Jesus

- Although Western text is wild, it is also very early

- Western text does not have an angrier Jesus elsewhere

- Verdict: Jesus was angry in Mark 1.41

Mark 1.41: Postscript

Why was Jesus angry?

- The ambiguity is in keeping with Mark's style

- More than a dozen reasons suggested

- Ehrman: Jesus was always angry when his desire/ability to heal was challenged

- Better: the leper came to the synagogue to be healed, and thus defiled the people there (Mark 1.39: "He went throughout Galilee preaching in their synagogues")

Only NIV 2011 & TNIV have an angry Jesus.

Some Famous Textual Problems:

John 5.3b–4, 1 Timothy 3.16, John 1.18

John 5.3b–4

- John 5.3–5, 7 in KJV: 3 In these lay a great multitude of impotent folk, of blind, halt, withered, waiting for the moving of the water. 4 For an angel went down at a certain season into the pool, and troubled the water: whosoever then first after the troubling of the water stepped in was made whole of whatsoever disease he had. 5 And a certain man was there, which had an infirmity thirty and eight years... 7 Sir, I have no man, when the water is troubled, to put me into the pool: but while I am coming, another steppeth down before me.

- John 5.3–5 in modern translations: 3 A great number of sick, blind, lame, and paralyzed people were lying in these walkways. 5 Now a man was there who had been disabled for thirty-eight years.

John 5.3b–4: Internal Evidence

Transcriptional probability:

- Unintentional change: only one possibility (see later discussion)
- Intentional change:

  o Some explanation seems to be called for; why would the lame man be at the pool?

  o Harder reading: no explanation for the lame man's statement in v. 7

  o Shorter reading: omit verses

Intrinsic probability:

- Style: Does not fit John's Greek syntax

- Style: Angels not prominent in John's Gospel

Only 1.51, 12.29, 20.12 (3x)

20x in Matthew, 5x in Mark, 25x in Luke

Internal grade: A– for shorter reading

John 5.3b–4: External Evidence

- Date & character:

  o   John 5.3b–4 absent in P66, ℵ, B, C*, D, many others

  o   John 5.3b–4 found in A, L, Itala, Byzantine MSS, several others

  o   Conclusion: earliest and best MSS lack the verses

- Genealogical solidarity:

  o   Absent: Alexandrian and best Western MSS

  o   Present: Byzantine and some Western, a couple late Alexandrian

  o   Conclusion: Alexandrian and Western lacked it, Byzantine had it

- Geographical distribution:

  o   Absent: Alexandrian and best Western MSS—widespread
          early on

  o   Present: Byzantine and some Western—widespread only
          later

External grade: solid A for omission

John 5.3b–4: other considerations

- Patristic writers: angel stirred up the waters

- Marginal note accidentally incorporated

- 1896: archeological evidence

- biblical principle(?): God helps those who help themselves

Conclusion: John 5.3b–4 is not authentic

Grade: A

Some Famous Textual Problems:

1 Timothy 3.16, John 1.18

1 Timothy 3.16

- KJV: "God was manifest in the flesh, justified in the Spirit, seen of angels, preached unto the Gentiles, believed on in the world, received up into glory."

- Modern translations:
  "He was revealed in the flesh, vindicated by the Spirit, seen by angels, proclaimed among Gentiles, believed on in the world, taken up in glory."

1 Timothy 3.16: Internal Evidence

Transcriptional probability:

Unintentional change:

Intentional change:

Intrinsic probability:

- Style: could go either way (Paul only rarely calls Jesus 'God')

- Style & context: poetry—often starts with relative pronoun (cf. Phil 2.6; Rom 4.25; Col 1.15; Heb 1.3)

Internal grade: A– for 'he'

1 Timothy 3.16: External Evidence

- Byzantine MSS: 'God'

- Best Alexandrian MSS: 'who' (with some being corrected by later hand:
א, A, C

- Western MSS: 'which' (Old Latin: quod)

1 Timothy 3.16: Conclusion

- 'he' is clearly authentic, confirmed by both external and internal evidence
- 'God' is an early orthodox corruption
- 'he' does not deny Christ's deity, nor does it explicitly affirm it
- Major text for KJV advocates: modern translations deny Christ's divinity!

John 1.18

- "No one has ever seen God. The unique one, himself God, who is in closest fellowship with the Father, has made God known"

- "No one has ever seen God; the only Son, who is in the bosom of the Father, he has made him known" (RSV)

- Variants: μονογενης θεος vs. μονογενης υιος
  o   monogenes theos vs. monogenes huios

- 'God': NET, NIV, TNIV, NIV 2011, ESV, NRSV, NASB

- 'Son': KJV, RV, ASV, RSV, HCSB, REB

John 1.18: Internal Evidence

Transcriptional probability:

- Unintentional error: possible, but depends on nomina sacra having either θC or YC

    o   Earliest NS were God, Christ, Lord, Jesus;

    o   Son was abbreviated later

    o   If θC is clearly a 2nd century reading, then accidental error is ruled out.

- Intentional error: no where else does John say 'the only one' followed by 'God'

    o   Three times John says 'the one and only Son': John 3.16, 18;
    1
             John 4.9

    o   John 3.16 loomed large in scribes' minds

    o   Text is not changed in John 3.16, 18, or 1 John 4.9

o   Grammar may have been misunderstood (see intrinsic evaluation)

Intrinsic probability:

• Ehrman: "when is an adjective ever used substantivally when it immediately precedes a noun of the same inflection?"

• His point: adjective + noun with matching case, gender, number = adjective modifies noun always

• Here, this would mean: "the one and only God" (Sabellianism)

Ehrman continues:

• "The result is that taking the term μονογενὴς θεός as two substantives standing in apposition makes for a nearly impossible syntax, whereas construing their relationship as adjective-noun creates an impossible sense."

• "To the best of my knowledge, no one has cited anything analogous outside of this passage."

• BUT there are several examples in NT (e.g., 2 Peter 2.5: "he preserved an eighth, Noah...")

• Context: monogenes used in John 1.14 substantivally ('the unique one')

• Thus: "the unique one, himself God"

- But it is just ambiguous enough that scribes may have misunderstood and thus changed the text to 'Son'

Internal grade: B for 'God'

John 1.18: External Evidence

- Alexandrian MSS: 'God'

  o   P66, P75, B, C*

- Western MSS: D is missing; Old Latin have 'Son'; א is Western in John 1–8 & it reads 'God'

- Byzantine MSS: 'Son'

- Geographical distribution:

  o   early church fathers have both readings

External grade: B for 'God'

John 1.18: Conclusion

- 'the unique one, himself God' is almost surely the authentic text and best way to translate it.

- Strong affirmation of Christ's deity; KJV has 'Son' instead of 'God'.

John 1.18 & 1 Timothy 3.16 & Christ's Divinity

- Do modern translations deny the deity of Christ? Not any more so than the KJV does:

- Both in text and translation KJV affirms Christ's divinity less than most modern translations. E.g.,

    o   Titus 2.13: "the glorious appearing of the great God and our Saviour Jesus Christ"

    o   2 Peter 1.1: "the righteousness of God and our Saviour Jesus Christ"

SESSION #32
SOME FAMOUS TEXTUAL PROBLEMS MATTHEW 24:36

TEXTUAL CRITICISM

Matthew 24.36
- Περὶ δὲ τῆς ἡμέρας ἐκείνης καὶ ὥρας οὐδεὶς οἶδεν, οὐδὲ οἱ ἄγγελοι τῶν οὐρανῶν οὐδὲ ὁ υἱός, εἰ μὴ ὁ πατὴρ μόνος.

- Now concerning that day and hour, no one knows it, neither the angels of heaven nor the Son, except the Father alone.

Matthew 24.36 & Bart Ehrman

- "The reason [for the omission] is not hard to postulate; if Jesus does not know the future, the Christian claim that he is a divine being is more than a little compromised."

- Misquoting Jesus, 204

- This is "the most famous instance" of doctrinal alteration by orthodox scribes

    - Studies in the Textual Criticism of the New Testament, 333

- "Scribes found this passage difficult: the Son of God, Jesus himself, does not know when the end will come? How could that be? Isn't he all-knowing? To resolve the problem, some scribes simply modified the text by taking out the words 'nor even the Son.' Now the angels may be ignorant, but the Son of God isn't."

    - Misquoting Jesus, 95

What if it wasn't the scribes who changed the text?

Arguments for Authenticity of
οὐδὲ ὁ υἱός ('nor the Son') in Matt 24.36:

1. External Evidence

א*, 2, B, D, Old Latin, Irenaeus, Origen,
 MSS acc. to Jerome

Matt 24.36 in א

Other Witnesses

- B: fourth-century Alexandrian majuscule

- D: early fifth-century Western majuscule

- ℵ *f*13: 9th century and later Caesarean witnesses

- majority of Old Latin witnesses (2nd century reading)

- Irlat: late 4th century translation of Irenaeus (late 2nd century Father); Irenaeus represents the Western text

- Origen: early to mid-third century Alexandrian witness

- MSS known to Jerome (late 4th/early 5th century)

Patristic Support for 'nor the Son'

- Irenaeus (late 2nd century) and Origen (early to mid-3rd century) apparently have the reading, and they show no awareness of the shorter reading.

- Their combined testimony suggests wide geographical distribution in the Western and Alexandrian regions from an early period

Arguments for Authenticity of 'nor the Son':

Internal Evidence

Metzger's Textual Commentary:

"The words 'neither the Son' are lacking in the majority of the witnesses of Matthew, including the later Byzantine text. On the other hand, the best representatives of the Alexandrian and the Western types of text contain the phrase. The omission of the words because of the doctrinal difficulty they present is more probable than their addition by assimilation to Mk 13.32. Furthermore, the presence of μόνος and the cast of the sentence as a whole (οὐδὲ ... οὐδέ ... belong together as a parenthesis...) suggest the originality of the phrase."

Two basic arguments:

1.   Grammar: strongly suggests authenticity of the words (correlative conjunctions)

2.   Theology: Scribes would be prone to omit these offensive words more than harmonize the text toward the parallel in Mark 13.32

Matthew 24.36 & Mark 13.32:
Parallel Passages

Matt 24.36: "Now concerning that day and hour, no one knows it, neither the angels of heaven nor the Son, except the Father alone."

Mark 13.32: "Now concerning that day or hour, no one knows it—neither the angels in heaven nor the Son—except the Father."

Arguments for Omission of 'nor the Son' in Matt 24.36:

1. External Evidence

ℵ1, L, W, *f*1, 33, Byz, Syriac, Coptic, Vulgate, Diatessaron, Athanasius, MSS acc. to Didymus, Phoebadius, MSS acc. to Ambrose, Basil, Gregory, MSS acc. to Jerome

Interpretation of Witnesses

- ℵ1: first corrector, 4th century, probably done before MS left scriptorium

- L: 8th century Alexandrian majuscule

- W: 4th/5th century Byzantine (in Matthew) majuscule

- *f*1: group of Caesarean minuscule

- 33: 'queen of the cursives': 9th century Alexandrian minuscule

- Byz: the Byzantine text-type

- Syriac: all Syriac witnesses (Western?), reaching back to 3rd century

- Coptic: all Coptic witnesses (strongly Alexandrian), reaching back to 3rd century

- MSS known to Jerome (late 4th/early 5th century) and preferred by Jerome (what he adopted in the Vulgate)

Other Patristic Support for the Omission

- Athanasius (late 3rd century, Alexandrian)
- Didymus (4th century, Alexandrian)
- Phoebadius (4th century, Western)
- Ambrose (4th century, Western)
- Jerome (4th-5th century, Western-Alexandrian)
- Basil (4th century, Byzantine)

The Fathers who favor the omission are relatively early and represent all three major text-forms.

Summary of external support for 'nor the Son'

- The best Alexandrian and Western witnesses

- This includes the earliest Alexandrian witness: ℵ*

- The second earliest Western witness (D) and the OL

- Some of the best Caesarean witnesses

- Early Fathers know of it, and some support it; some know only of this reading

- The evidence is widespread, early, and in important witnesses

Summary of external support for omission

- Decent Alexandrian and Western witnesses, including the earliest Alexandrian version (Sahidic Coptic—3rd century) and an early Western version (Syriac)

- The earliest Greek witness: ℵ1 (primary Alexandrian)

- Some of the best Caesarean witnesses

- Relatively early and important fathers

- The evidence is widespread, early, and in important witnesses

- But it is not the reading of all the earliest and best Alexandrian and Western witnesses.

Summary of External Evidence

Although the external evidence is by no means rock-solid for either reading, the weight must be given to the longer reading. οὐδὲ ὁ υἱός is early, widespread, and found in the better witnesses overall. But a decision is difficult.

Conclusion:

C+/B– rating in favor of longer reading

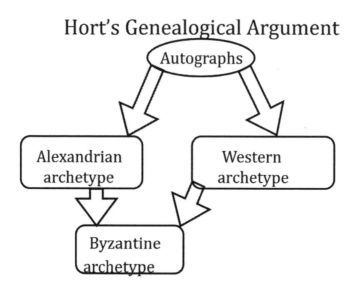

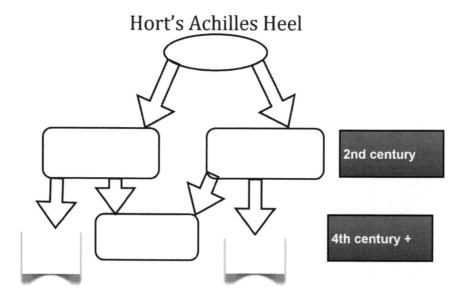

Implications of Hort's Achilles' Heel

On rare occasions, the Byzantine text can have the original wording by itself—especially when it has the shorter reading; When supported by other early witnesses, a Byzantine authentic reading is even more possible.

Arguments for Authenticity of 'nor the Son':

Internal Evidence:

2. Intrinsic Probability

- Grammar: 'neither the angels... nor the Son': Are the correlative conjunctions a grammatical necessity (so Ehrman, Orthodox Corruption, 92)? Put simply:

- Does neither demand a nor afterward?

Arguments for Authenticity of οὐδὲ ὁ υἱός:
Internal Evidence

- Counter-grammatical argument:

- Although oude is often used in pairs, it is not at all required to do so.

- Matthew has 27 instances of oude; the only paired instance is in Matt 12.19 (quoting OT).

- oude by itself means 'not, not even.' The sentence makes good sense with only one oude.

Arguments for Authenticity of 'nor the Son':
Internal Evidence

- Theology: 'nor the Son' offensive to a high Christology and thus most scribes omitted the words.

- So most commentators today, largely influenced by Metzger

Arguments for Authenticity of οὐδὲ ὁ υἱός:
Internal Evidence

- Theology continued: The omission is an anti-Adoptionistic reading (Ehrman, Orthodox Corruption)

- Adoptionism thrived AD 190–275; anti-Adoptionist sentiment was correspondingly vigorous during that time

- Third century fathers would be most likely to have altered the text that the scribes then copied

Arguments for Authenticity of 'nor the Son':
Internal Evidence

- Theology concluded: How is the parallel in Mark 13.32 to be explained where the words 'nor the Son' are certain?

- Mark was copied less frequently than Matthew; scribes almost always conformed Mark to Matthew rather than vice versa.

Arguments for Authenticity of οὐδὲ ὁ υἱός:
Internal Evidence

- Theology counter-arguments:
proto-orthodox response to Adoptionism would be long after all four
Gospels were considered canonical (Irenaeus, Against Heresies 3.11.8)

How could the proto-orthodox alter Matthew while neglecting to do so in
Mark? The same MSS that omit the phrase in Matthew have it in Mark.

Arguments for Authenticity of 'nor the Son':
Internal Evidence

- Theology counter-argument:
Patristic evidence: No church father had any problem with 'nor the
Son' until the 4th century—long ager the Adoptionist controversy was
over.

Thus, the Adoptionist controversy seems to be irrelevant to this textual
problem.

Arguments for Omitting 'nor the Son':
Internal Evidence

Theology vs. Harmonization: If omission is due to anti-Adoptionistic
views, it arose after all four Gospels were considered canonical: Why, then,
is 'nor the Son' not omitted in Mark?

Harmonization sometimes trumps theology—even Matthew harmonizing
toward Mark:

Mark 10.17–18: "Good teacher, what must I do to inherit eternal life?" Jesus said, "Why do you call me good? No one is good but God alone."

Matt 19.16–17: "Teacher, what good thing must I do to have eternal life?" "Why do you ask me about the good? Only one is good."

- The problem of Matthew's μόνος (alone) for scribal corruption:

  Why did they leave 'alone' alone?

  But would Matthew leave 'alone' in the text?

Christology in Matthew and Mark

Mark 1.12: Spirit <u>drove</u> Jesus into wilderness	Matt 4.1: Spirit <u>led</u> Jesus into wilderness	*Jesus' will*
Mark 2.26: Jesus spoke of David entering house of God <u>when Abiathar was high priest</u>	Matt 12.4: 'when Abiathar was high priest' is omitted: it was Ahimelech who was priest...	*Jesus' knowledge*
Mark 3.10: Jesus healed <u>many</u>	Matt 12.15: Jesus healed them <u>all</u>	*Jesus' power*

Christology in Matthew and Mark

Mark 5.30–32: Jesus knew that power had gone out from him; 'Who touched me?'	Matt 9.18–26: both points omitted	*Jesus' power, knowledge*
Mark 6.5: <u>not able</u> to do any miracle in his hometown... except...	Matt 13.58: <u>did not</u> do many miracles	*Jesus' power*
Mark 6.6: Jesus was <u>amazed</u> at their unbelief	Matthew omits	*Jesus' knowledge*

Christology in Matthew and Mark

Mark 8.22–26: healing blind man with spittle—twice	Matthew omits this pericope entirely	*Jesus' power*

Christology in Matthew and Mark

Matthew never has a lower Christology when it comes to Jesus' holiness, will, power, knowledge, emotions, disciples' derived authority from Jesus, or worship of Jesus.

Verdict:

Matthew, not later scribes, omitted 'nor the Son' from his Gospel, and replaced it with 'alone.' He softened the statement of the Son's ignorance, making what was explicit now implicit. In the least, the plausibility of Matthew, rather than the scribes, omitting the phrase, calls into question Bart Ehrman's claims of extensive and significant proto-orthodox corruption of scripture. Yet, if Matthew changed the text, he nevertheless retained the gist of what the Lord said. His 'alone' concerning the Father's knowledge implies what Mark's 'nor the Son' explicitly says.

Thus, the Gospel writers may change the words of Jesus, but they still retain the gist of what he said.

.

SESSION #33

SOME FAMOUS TEXTUAL PROBLEMS JOHN 7:53-8:11

TEXTUAL CRITICISM

My favorite passage that's not in the Bible:

A distinction needs to be made between what is canonical and what is historical

- Is it possible for a story about Jesus to be true without it being part of the New Testament?

- Respect for the author requires that we investigate dubious passages seriously

- The incarnation gives us a methodological imperative to do serious historical research

- A distinction needs to be made between what is canonical and what is historical

- More emotional baggage is attached to the PA than to any other passage in the New Testament

- If it is not part of the NT, what do we lose?

- This pericope may well be true historically even if John did not write it

- An examination of the evidence is therefore in order

John 7.53–8.11

- External evidence

  o   Lacking in P66, P75, ℵ, B, A, C, and almost all MSS through 8th century

  o   Only three majuscules have it: D, K, ℵ

  o   Earliest and best versions lack it

- o   Lack of patristic comments until 12th century

- o   Asterisks in several MSS

- o   Corruptions within pericope adulterae

- o   Floating text

- o   Three locations within John 7

- o   After all four Gospels

- o   Between Luke and John

- o   After John 8.12

- o   After Luke 21.38

- Internal evidence

  - o   Vocabulary, syntax, style not John's

  - o   No other pericope so anomalous

- o   Disrupts the passage

- o   Language is similar to Luke's

John 7.53–8.11 and Luke

- Kyle R. Hughes, "The Lukan Special Material and the Tradition History of the Pericope Adulterae," Novum Testamentum 55 (2013) 232–51

- Finally, the mystery of its origin may have been discovered.

Syntax, style, vocabulary similar to Luke's 'special' material

- Recent excavations reveal two different versions of the story, con flating in the third century

- Did Luke have access to one of them?

- Several features in the PA are found in Luke's special material: un named woman, historical presents, verb forms

- Why, then, did he not include it in his Gospel?

Conclusion

- PA almost surely not authentic

- Mark 16 & John 8: MS evidence compared

- Pastor & early MSS

- Ehrman's Misquoting Jesus and the PA; Gibbon's Decline and Fall of the Roman Empire and 1 John 5.7

Epilogue: Incarnation and Inspiration

- Priority: Incarnation or inspiration?

- Yet we cannot know Jesus apart from the scriptures.

- However, even if the Bible were not inspired this would not mean it was historically worthless.

- The incarnation demands of us historical research, while many evangelicals' views of inerrancy argues against this.

- What will triumph in the end?

SESSION #34
SOME FAMOUS TEXTUAL PROBLEMS MARK 16:9-20

TEXTUAL CRITICISM

When the End is not the End: The Conclusion to Mark's Gospel

There are five different endings to the Gospel of Mark. Which one, if any, concluded the Gospel?

1. The Gospel Ends at 16.8 (short ending or SE):

Then they [Mary Magdalene, Mary the mother of James, and Salome] went out and ran from the tomb, for terror and bewilderment had seized them. And they said nothing to anyone, because they were afraid.

2. Intermediate Ending (IE) after v. 8:

But they reported briefly to Peter and those with him all that they had been told. And after these things Jesus himself sent out through them, from east to west, the sacred and imperishable proclamation of eternal salvation.

3. IE followed by Long Ending (LE)

The LE:

> (9) Early on the first day of the week, after he arose, he appeared first to Mary Magdalene, from whom he had driven out seven demons. (10) She went out and told those who were with him, while they were mourning and weeping. (11) And when they heard that he was alive and had been seen by her, they did not believe. (12) After this he appeared in a different form to two of them while they were on their way to the country. (13) They went back and told the rest, but they did not believe them. (14) Then he appeared to the eleven themselves, while they were eating, and he rebuked them for their unbelief and hardness of heart, because they did not believe those who had seen him resurrected. (15) He said to them, "Go into all the world and preach the gospel to every creature. (16) The one who believes and is baptized will be saved, but the one who does not believe will be condemned. (17) These signs will accompany those who believe: In my name they will drive out demons; they will speak in new languages; (18) they will pick up snakes with their hands, and whatever poison they drink will not harm them; they will place their hands on the sick and they will be well." (19) After the Lord Jesus had spoken to them, he was taken up into heaven and sat down at the right hand of God. (20) They went out and proclaimed everywhere, while the Lord worked with them and confirmed the word through the accompanying signs.

5. LE with material added between vv. 14 and 15 (Freer Logion):

And they excused themselves, saying, "This age of lawlessness and unbelief is under Satan, who does not allow the truth and power of God to prevail over the unclean things of the spirits. Therefore reveal your righteousness now"—thus they spoke to Christ. And Christ replied to them, "The term of years of Satan's power has been fulfilled, but other terrible things draw near. And for those who have sinned I was handed over to death, that they may return to the truth and sin no more, in order that they may inherit the spiritual and incorruptible glory of righteousness that is in heaven."

Summary of External Evidence

Three endings can be eliminated: IE, IE followed by LE, and Freer Logion between vv. 14–15 of LE

This leaves two endings: SE and LE. Which is more likely—that scribes would intentionally omit vv. 9–20 or that they would add these verses?

Arguments for LE:

- At least 95% of all MSS, versions, and Fathers

- Found as early as the late fourth/early fifth century (codex W—the Freer MS)

- All three text-forms: Byzantine, Western, Alexandrian (geographical distribution)

- Fathers (beginning no later than the late second century [with Irenaeus])

- Why would these verses be omitted by scribes?

- embarrassment over vv. 17–18 (snakes, poison)?

- But at least ten fathers quote from or allude to vv. 15-20 in a steady stream from the second to the fifth century, while no fathers mention the first half of the pericope (vv. 9–14) until the fourth century.

- The evidence reveals that the fathers did not have a problem with vv. 17–18.

Arguments for short ending:

Scribes would be strongly tempted to add a resurrection appearance to this Gospel:

8.31, 9.9, 9.31, 10.34—predictions of the resurrection of Jesus

Only Gospel that doesn't have a resurrection appearance by Jesus to the disciples

(Sinaiticus: 4th century): ℵ

(Vaticanus: 4th century): B

These are the best witnesses to the most important text-type: the Alexandrian

3000 differences in Gospels argues for common ancestor several generations back, probably deep in the 2nd century

The blank column at the end of Mark in codex B is the only blank column in the NT of B

Does this indicate that the scribe knew of the LE and was making room for it?

- Unlikely because there's not enough room for the LE

- Unlikely because the three OT blank columns are at the end of a genre

This suggests that B's archetype had Mark at the end of the four Gospels (Western order, like W and D have)

Acts would come next—a different genre

Other evidence that B's archetype had a different order of books: Paul's epistles are in a different order than the archetype (paragraph numbering shows displacement)

If the blank column in B indicates that the scribe was aware of the LE, what does the blank PAGE at the end of the Gospels in Sinaiticus indicate?

The oldest Syriac, Armenian, Georgian, and Sahidic manuscripts end the Gospel at v. 8. Syriac (Sinaitic): text-form from 2nd century; ends at v. 8.

They represent early and wide distribution.

Origen and Clement (2nd and 3rd century) are silent about any material after v. 8.

Eusebius (early 4th century): "The accurate copies conclude the story according to Mark in the words... 'they were afraid' for the end is here in nearly all the copies of Mark."

Jerome (end of fourth/beginning of fifth century): the LE is found in "scarcely any copies of the Gospel—almost all the Greek codices being without this passage..."

Victor of Antioch (fifth–sixth century): both endings were in wide circulation, but Victor believed the longer ending was more accurate. Victor wrote the most popular commentary on Mark of the Middle Ages.

It may well have been due to his influence that scribes added the LE from then on.

Alternative endings:

• Codex Bobiensis (c. 400 CE): the IE, a colorless ending. If the LE was known to the scribe, why would he omit it and use instead a bland ending?

• Several manuscripts and versions from the fourth to ninth century have the IE before the LE. None have the IE after the LE. This shows that some of their ancestors had only the IE, and later scribes added the LE after it.

"No one who had available as the conclusion of the second Gospel the twelve verses 9–20, so rich in interesting material, would have deliberately replaced them with a few lines of a colorless and generalized summary."
                                        - Bruce Metzger, Textual Commentary

Marginal notes:

Even in many of the MSS that have the LE, there is a note that registers suspicion: "The end. In some copies the evangelist ended here, but in many this also"—referring to vv. 9–20 which follow.

Others have "Eusebius canonized the Gospel to here" (referring to v. 8).

Others have asterisks after v. 8, indicating doubt about authenticity.

- Why does this Gospel, and only this gospel, have major textual upheaval at the end?

- Because scribes were uncomfortable with a gospel ending without any resurrection appearances.

- If Mark 16.9–20 were original, then why would the material be deleted? Why don't any MSS delete the endings of Mt, Lk, or Jn?

Conclusion of external evidence:

The manuscripts, versions, and patristic writings on behalf of the SE are early and widespread. They represent the Alexandrian, Western, Caesarean, and Byzantine text-types. The SE is found in the best witnesses of the three most important early versions—Latin, Coptic, and Syriac—as well as the best and earliest witnesses of the Armenian and Georgian. It is also found in the best witnesses of the Alexandrian, Caesarean, and Western text.

Eusebius and Jerome, whose access to MSS was vast, both affirm that the SE was by far the predominant conclusion to Mark in their day.

The reason for later MSS to have some ending after 16.8 is easily explainable (scribal desire to have a resurrection appearance by Jesus to the disciples), while no convincing reason has been proposed as to why some scribes should eliminate vv. 9–20.

Internal Evidence:

Both transcriptional (scribal) and intrinsic (authorial) evidence argue decisively against the authenticity of the LE.

- Transcriptional: we have seen that scribes would be more likely to add material after 16.8 than delete it.

- Intrinsic evidence: there is not a single passage in Mark 1.1–16.8 comparable to the stylistic, grammatical, and lexical anomalies that we find clustered in 16.9–20.

See Gregory Sapaugh, "An Appraisal of the Intrinsic Probability of the Longer Endings of the Gospel of Mark" (PhD dissertation, Dallas Theological Seminary, 2012)

Did Mark intentionally end his Gospel at 16.8 or is the ending lost?

Three arguments that ending was lost:

1. Last leaf could have been lost if written on a codex

2. Books don't end in a γάρ ('for')

3. Open-ended conclusions are a modern Kafka-like invention

Three counter-arguments:

1. Mark would have been written on a roll, and the end is the most protected leaf

2. Books have been discovered that end in a γάρ

3. Open-ended conclusions are ancient

Three counter-arguments:

1. roll vs. codex: see T. C. Skeat and C. H. Roberts, The Birth of the Codex (OUP, 1987): Mark was written on a roll, not a codex

2. Books ending in a γάρ: see P. W. van der Horst, "Can a Book End with a ΓΑΡ? A Note on Mark XVI.8," JTS 23 (1972) 121-24; Kelly R. Iverson, "A Further Word on Final Γάρ (Mark 16:8)," CBQ 68 (2006) 79-94

3. Open-ended conclusions are ancient: J. Lee Magness, Marking the End: Sense and Absence in the Gospel of Mark (Atlanta: Scholars, 1986)

Open-ended conclusions are ancient:

- Some Greco-Roman literature is open-ended

- Several OT passages are open-ended

- Even a whole book, Jonah, ends this way

Mark seems to foreshadow the ἐφοβοῦντο γάρ of 16.8 with the open-ended conclusion to the pericope of Jesus' third prediction about his resurrection in 9.32: "But they did not understand this statement and were afraid to ask him [ἐφοβοῦντο]."

Significantly, this foreshadows Mark 16.8 in five ways:

1. It deals with Jesus' resurrection

2. The pericope is open-ended

3. The verb is an imperfect, which by its nature is open-ended

4. It is the same verb (and form) as used in 16.8

5. The pericope ends with the disciples bewildered

But why did no one in the ancient world understand Mark's intention?

Luke apparently did: The conclusion to Acts is open-ended

- "No one can accept the ending of Acts as the conclusion of a rationally conceived history" (W. R. Ramsey, St. Paul the Traveller and Roman Citizen) 321–22.

- Luke seems to have a similar purpose: get the reader involved in the narrative.

- Acts starts with a bang and ends with a whimper, leaving the reader wanting more.

Does Luke give any other clues that he is emulating Mark's literary technique?

The beginning of Acts...

"I wrote the former account, Theophilus, about all that Jesus began to do and teach until the day he was taken up to heaven..."

- Compare this with the beginning of Mark:

- "The beginning of the gospel of Jesus Christ, the Son of God."

- Often the first line in an ancient book was meant to be the title. If this is so here, Mark's Gospel gives a sufficient clue that 16.8 is the real ending.

- Luke picked up on this and spoke of his Gospel as the beginning of what Jesus did.

- Acts continues the narrative, but leaves off for the reader to get engaged in spreading the gospel.

Conclusion

Although at first glance the evidence is overwhelming on behalf of the LE, a more penetrating analysis reveals:

- the earliest and best manuscripts and versions, with the greatest geographical spread;
- the comments by Eusebius and Jerome about the majority of manuscripts in their day ending at v. 8;
- the multitude of endings before or in place of the LE;
- the marginal notes in the manuscripts complaining about the LE;
- and the overwhelming evidence from the linguistic uniqueness of the passage—all argue that Mark ended his Gospel at 16.8.

Why does Mark complete his Gospel this way? It's an invitation to the reader...

Mark's challenge to his readers in his day is still valid today: What are you going to do with Jesus?

For more information see:

Daniel B. Wallace, "Mark 16:8 as the Conclusion to the Second Gospel," in Perspectives on the Ending of Mark: Four Views, ed. D. A. Black (Nashville: B&H Academic, 2008) 1–39.

SESSION #35

WHY SO MANY VERSIONS? WHAT TRANSLATION IS BEST?

TEXTUAL CRITICISM

Three major influences behind modern translations:

1. New text to translate from (1881+)
2. New information about language of NT (1895+)
3. New philosophies of translation (20th century)

Thus: textual, informational, and philosophical changes are behind the modern translations

The Text of Modern Translations

- Textual basis: older MSS, better MSS

(Westcott-Hort)

- Informational basis: discovery of papyri (Deissmann), linguistic studies, exegetical studies

- Translational theory: formal equivalent vs. functional equivalent—and more!

Basic Principles in Translation

Translation Philosophy: Three Priorities

1. Elegance
2. Accuracy
3. Readability

Basic Principles in Translation

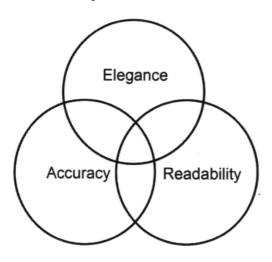

What's the Best Translation?
A Brief Examination of Some Contenders

- NIV (1984)

- RSV (1952, 1971)

- NASB (1960, 1995)

- ESV (2008)

- REB (1989)

- NKJV (1982)

- NET (2005)

- NIV 2011 (2011)

What about Gender-Inclusive Language?

- RSV and Isa 7.14

- NRSV, NIV 2011 and some passages

- Matt 18.15: "If your brother or sister sins, go and point out their fault, just between the two of you. If they listen to you, you have won them over" (NIV 2011).

- "If another member of the church sins against you, go and point out the fault when the two of you are alone. If the member listens to you, you have regained that one" (NRSV).

- 1 Tim 3.2: "Now the overseer is to be above reproach, faithful to his wife, temperate, self-controlled, hospitable, able to teach" (NIV 2011).

- "Now a bishop must be above reproach, married only once, temperate, sensible, respectable, hospitable, an apt teacher" (NRSV).

What Bibles Should I Read?

- King James Bible

- Good study Bible: NET, ESV, NIV 2011

- Good reading Bible: NIV 2011, REB, NLT, The Message

- Good memorizing Bible: ESV, KJV, NET

Final thoughts

All translation is interpretation.

The differences among these translations are important, but not essential for salvation.

The Spirit of God has ensured that the truth of the scriptures can be found in any one of them.

Each believer has the right and the responsibility to read the Bible in his/her own language, and to grapple in the community of believers with what it means and how it should be obeyed.

Tolle lege!

SESSION #36

IS WHAT WE HAVE NOW WHAT THEY WROTE THEN?

TEXTUAL CRITICISM

Atheists are joining the chorus:

> "We do not have any of the original manuscripts of the Bible. The
> originals are lost. We don't know when and we don't know by whom.
> What we have are copies of copies. In some instances, the copies we
> have are twentieth generation copies."
>
> - C. J. Werleman, Jesus Lied, p. 41.

And Muslims, too:

> "The Orthodox Church, being the sect which eventually established su-
> premacy over all the others, stood in fervent opposition to various ideas
> ([a.k.a.] 'heresies') which were in circulation. These included Adoption-

ism (the notion that Jesus was not God, but a man); Docetism (the opposite view, that he was God and not man); and Separationism (that the divine and human elements of Jesus Christ were two separate beings). In each case this sect, the one that would rise to become the Orthodox Church, deliberately corrupted the Scriptures so as to reflect its own theological visions of Christ, while demolishing that of all rival sects."

M. M. Al-Azami, The History of the Qur'anic Text from Revelation to Compilation: a Comparative Study with the Old and New Testaments, p. 277.

"Not only do we not have the originals, we don't have the first copies of the originals. We don't even have copies of the copies of the originals, or copies of the copies of the copies of the originals."

- Bart Ehrman, Misquoting Jesus

Has the New Testament text been corrupted?

Yes of course. But how badly?

Two attitudes to avoid

1. Radical skepticism

2. Absolute Certainty

Four Questions to Answer

1. How many textual variants are there?

2. What kinds of textual variations are there?

3. What theological beliefs depend on textually suspect passages?

4. Is what we have now what they wrote then?

Preliminary question: Don't we have the original New Testament anymore?

Number of Variants

Textual variant- Any place among the manuscripts in which there is variation in wording, including word order, omission or addition of words, even spelling differences

The Quantity of Variants

Greek NT:
c. 140,000

Textual Variants:
c. 400,000

The reason we have a lot of textual variants is that we have a lot of manuscripts.

Richard Bentley,
Remarks upon a Discourse of Free Thinking (1713)

> "If there had been but one manuscript of the Greek Testament at the restoration of learning about two centuries ago, then we [would have] had no various readings at all. ... And would the text be in a better condition then, than now [that] we have 30,000 [variant readings]? It is good, therefore... to have more anchors than one; and another MS. to join the first would give more authority, as well as security."

An Embarrassment of Riches

- Greek manuscripts: 5824

- Latin manuscripts: 10,000+

- Other ancient versions: 5000–10,000

- Quotations from the New Testament by church fathers: over 1 million

The NT compared to the average classical work

- The average classical Greek writer has less than 20 copies of his works still in existence.

- Stack them up, and they're 4 feet high.

The NT compared to the average classical work

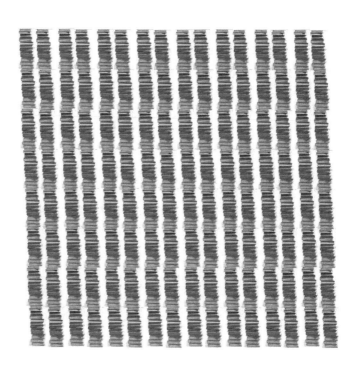

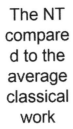

Greco-Roman authors

- Pliny the Elder: 700 years

- Plutarch: 800 years

- Josephus: 800 years

- Polybius: 1200 years

- Pausanias: 1400 years

- Herodotus: 1500 years

- Xenophon: 1800 years

The Date of NT MSS

The Discovery of P52

An ounce of evidence is worth a pound of presumption!

Has the Bible been translated and retranslated so many times that we don't know what it originally said?

Year	Number of MSS	Earliest MSS
1611	7	11th century
2013	5800+	2nd century

The bottom line

As time goes on, we are getting closer and closer to the original text.

The nature of the variants: What kinds of variants are there?

- 99% make virtually no difference at all.
- For example:

    o   differences in spellign
    o   differences in spelling

The smallest group of variants:

- Meaningful and viable (good chance of being authentic)
- Less than 1% of all textual variants fit this group.

    Mark 9.29: "This kind [of demon] cannot be cast out except by prayer [and fasting.]"

    Revelation 13.18—"Let the one who has insight calculate the beast's number, for it is the number of a man, and his number is 666."

What theological beliefs depend on textually suspect passages?

An ounce of evidence is worth a pound of presumption.
P66 (c. AD 175)

Unnatural Seuge

- Polar bear attacks man in Canada and bystanders do nothing.

    The media did not even report this incident!

Appendix to Bart Ehrman's Misquoting Jesus

"Why do you believe these core tenets of Christian orthodoxy to be in jeopardy based on the scribal errors you discovered in the biblical manuscripts?"

Ehrman's response:

> "Essential Christian beliefs are not affected by textual variants in the manuscript tradition of the New Testament."

Is What We Have Now What They Wrote Then?

In all particulars?
Probably not.

But in all essentials?
Absolutely.

No essential doctrine of the Christian faith is jeopardized by any viable variant.